FIRST TIME TENANT

Also available

First Time Buyer: First Time Seller
Getting the Builders In
The Law in Brief

FIRST TIME TENANT

Patricia Barber

RIGHT WAY

Typeset in 11 pt Times by Letterpart Ltd., Reigate, Surrey.
Printed and bound in Great Britain by Cox & Wyman Ltd., Reading, Berkshire.

The *Right Way* series is published by Elliot Right Way Books, Brighton Road, Lower Kingswood, Tadworth, Surrey, KT20 6TD, U.K. For information about our company and the other books we publish, visit our website at www.right-way.co.uk

DEDICATION

To Paul, Jenny and Helen
for their continuing love and support.

Also to everyone involved in the business of lettings: may
all your problems be smaller from now on!

CONTENTS

INTRODUCTION

The lettings market has never been more buoyant. More and more people are investing in additional property to bring in extra income; sadly very few of these new landlords have a clue about how to treat their tenants.

The number of tenant/landlord disputes has risen sharply over the last few years. In just one recent year, there were more than 300,000 disputes with around 60 per cent of these moving into the court system.

I have worked in the lettings industry for more than twenty years and have heard some frightening tales told to me by tenants who have run into trouble with landlords, letting agents and even their own housemates. Not everyone is out to rip you off but, when renting property, it does pay to be informed and try to stay ahead of the game.

'Buy-to-let' has had a massive effect on the housing market and while prospective landlords are awash with information and advice, it seems that the tenant, without whom there would be no lettings market, is left high and dry. With this book I hope to redress the balance and provide a whole host of useful information without the complicated legal jargon that usually confuses rather than informs.

Throughout the book you will find lots of useful common sense tips, special notes for students and real case histories to illustrate some of the problems that occur during just about every tenancy but which can easily be avoided and save you money.

This book is not intended to be a completely comprehensive and legal guide, it aims to be informative and offer useful insights to anyone thinking of moving into a rented property. If you find yourself in a problematic situation you should always consult a solicitor or other suitably qualified adviser.

1

THINKING OF RENTING?

Reasons to Rent

There are many reasons why you may be thinking of renting somewhere to live. You could be going to university or leaving home for the first time, moving because of work or family commitments, or maybe your house is suffering from subsidence or flooding and you need somewhere to live temporarily until repair work is completed. You may, of course, simply have sold your own property and want to take your time to find just the right property to buy.

In any of these situations renting is a good plan and an easy option that allows you to stay in one place for around six months. This is a relatively short time during which you can decide whether this is the right place for you, whether you wish to stay longer or simply move on to another property which is of better quality or in a more convenient location.

Lettings of less than six months are rare but not unheard of. If, for example, your circumstances dictate that you only need to stay in a property for three months, and provided the landlord agrees, letting agents will be able to draw up an *Assured Shorthold Agreement* with a 'get out' clause (called a *Break Clause*). This ensures that both you and the landlord are legally protected and allows you to leave when you need to.

However, if your circumstances change during the tenancy, you can lawfully stay for the full six months and the landlord cannot evict you before the end of that time.

To Share or Not To Share
Your own personal circumstances will usually dictate whether you decide to go it alone or share a house or flat with other people. Both have their plus points but there are also drawbacks. You need to think carefully about your situation, your finances and how you like to live your life before you commit yourself. If you are an independent kind of person who is quite happy with your own company, spend long hours studying or working from home or just like to live a quiet, hermit-like existence then obviously sharing may not work for you. However, if you are a sociable and out-going kind of soul who mixes well with others and who has a flexible attitude then sharing will probably not be a problem.

Shared/Joint Tenancies
When you are thinking of renting you could find that there are others in your circle who are also in the same position and it could be a good idea to get together and pool your resources. The main benefit of sharing is that together you will be able to afford a bigger, better property and this will allow you to have a better choice from what is available. Smaller one and two bedroomed places to rent are at a premium and can get snapped up almost as soon as they appear on the market. Sharing a flat or house with other people can either work very well or leave you with a big headache depending on how you have approached things. Other people bring their own problems into a tenancy; it's not unlike being married in many ways, so you need to look at things very carefully before you commit yourself to sharing your new home with other people. There are several plus points about sharing:

● You will only need to find your own portion of the security deposit

- All the household expenses will be shared between tenants

- Being responsible for running a whole property is serious business; you will have the security of knowing that these responsibilities can be shared. Small things like fuses blowing or a blocked sink don't seem quite so hard to deal with when someone else is there to help

- You will never be lonely!

However, there are a couple of drawbacks and these should be thought about very carefully before you get too carried away with the thought of all those house parties.

- How well do you know your prospective housemates? On a personal level you need to know, for example, if they have any annoying habits. Is their personal hygiene as good as your own? Living closely with someone else, on a daily basis, can be a nightmare if you also have to live with his or her disgusting habits. Leaving smelly socks about the place is unpleasant as well as untidy!

- Do you really know much about their financial situation? You need to be sure that they will be able to pay their rent and share of household expenses on time – all the time.

All tenants are 'jointly and severally' responsible for the rent payments and utilities, which means that the landlord or his agent expects 100 per cent of the rent to be paid every month, on time, regardless of your internal housemates' problems.

All your prospective housemates should know just what their responsibilities are at the start. If one of them decides to leave at some point during the tenancy, the total monthly rent is still payable no matter how many of the tenants are living in the property.

Sole Tenancy
Perhaps you are in the happy position of being able to afford to rent a property on your own. If you are content with your own company and do not want to share your living space with others there are many benefits in becoming a sole tenant.

- You won't be disturbed by anyone else late at night or early in the morning

- You only have your own mess and bad habits to deal with

- You don't have to depend on anyone else to pay all the bills and therefore know when and if they are paid

- You will never have the worry of a housemate deciding to leave half way through the tenancy

- You have control over how much you are paying out; you can ensure that the heating is turned off when needed; and that your telephone bill is not spiralling out of control.

However, on the minus side of things you will have to find 100 per cent of the large security deposit needed at the start of the tenancy (up to the equivalent of one and a half months' rent is usually required) and you alone will be responsible for the payment of all the rent and household bills – unless you can call on the services of a generous fairy godmother or father! You will be on your own if the power supply fails or you accidentally flood the bathroom.

Assessing Your Finances
Before you start searching your local letting agencies and property papers, you should work out how much you can

afford. Even if you will be sharing the house with your partner or friends or relatives, you need to sit down and calculate just how much rent you can jointly afford to pay. This is not as simple as it sounds. Think about your whole budget. What other expenses do you have? There's council tax, utility bills, basic living expenses, your entertainment budget . . .

Information Point

Letting agents have a simple calculation for working out how much salary you will need to earn to cover your rental obligations. The usual requirement is that the tenant(s) must earn an annual salary or combined salaries equivalent to 30 times the monthly rental cost.

For example: if the rent is to be £500 per calendar month the ideal annual salary needed would be £15,000 per year (£500 x 30). If these figures do not quite match then you may be asked to provide six months' rent in advance or to provide the name and address of a guarantor. The agency will then carry out the same financial checks on the guarantor.

Monthly Council Tax Payment

Council tax is charged under a banding system, depending on the area and value of the property. At the time of writing, the bands are graded from A to H and charges are calculated according to the market value of the property at 1st April 1991.

The landlord or letting agent should have the information you will need regarding council tax payments due on the property you're interested in. If they don't, it is very easy to find out for yourself by simply calling the local district council and asking for the council tax payments office. You'll need to quote the address and/or postcode of the property and then they will be able to tell you exactly how much you'll need to pay.

COUNCIL TAX DISCOUNTS

There is a *25 per cent discount* for sole occupancy so if you intend to rent on your own, you need to inform the council in order to get your discount. If you are registered as disabled and are renting a property that has been converted for your use, there is a large range of discounts available and these vary from council to council.

Notes for Students

You are exempt from paying council tax if all the occupants of a property are in full time education. You will probably be asked to provide a certificate giving evidence of your student status. You can get this from your faculty office after you have registered for a course.

If any of the above discounts applies, you will need to inform your local council tax office of your circumstances otherwise you will be charged automatically for the full amount due.

PAYMENT METHODS

Among the various ways of paying council tax, some or all of the following (and others) may be available in your area:

● Direct Debit: via ten monthly instalments through your bank account

- Post Office: via a plastic swipe card that your council tax office will send you

- Cheque or Cash: payable monthly via the bank payment book that the council tax office will give you.

Other Utility Bills
GAS AND ELECTRICITY

These can also be paid on a monthly direct debit through your bank account or when each quarterly bill comes in you can collect each housemate's share and pay either by posting a cheque or paying by cash at the bank or post office.

When a tenant has not held a utility account before then the electricity or gas company may suggest that you have a card meter installed. This is the modern version of the 'money-in-the-slot' type meter that was popular many years ago. The utility company will issue you with a long black plastic 'key' for which you will have to pay a small amount of money (say £10). The key will be charged/credited with electricity or gas to the total amount paid by you. You will then need to insert this key into the meter in your property. The meter display will show you how much credit you have.

Keep an eye on the meter reading, when this reduces you will need to recharge your key, otherwise you will end up with no lights, heating, hot water or power for cooking. You can recharge by taking the key to one of a number of local shops or petrol stations who act as agents for gas and electricity companies. Your service company will be able to give you information about the location of these sites. The shop/agent will have a swipe machine which will recharge your key for any amount of credit you care to pay. The only golden rule when dealing with key meters is that you should keep an emergency credit of no less than £5 at all times. When you leave the property at the end of the tenancy this credit should be present.

WATER CHARGES
These will vary throughout the country. Many of the more modern properties will have a water meter which means you will only pay for the water that you use during your tenancy. Your bill is calculated on the number of units used by reading the meter in the same way as your gas and electricity meters are read. The alternative is an annual charge, either payable in two six-monthly instalments or eight monthly direct debit payments.

Some letting agents ensure that the landlord pays all water charges on a non-metered property, others include this in the tenancy agreement as a tenant's responsibility.

You will need to find out just what the position is before you move in.

TELEPHONE
Do you need a 'landline'? As most people seem to have their own mobile phone many tenants do not have a regular telephone line connected. If your mobile is too expensive and you need a normal telephone line in the house, you should find out if this is already in place and, if so, is it disconnected?

If the line is in place and 'live', you may just need to transfer the account to your name. If the line is disconnected, the charges to re-connect will be much higher than for a name transfer.

- If you are moving into a brand new property where no line has yet been installed, a fee is payable

- If the last occupier has simply cancelled his account with BT, the reconnection is FREE

- If the line has been unused for a long period of time, an engineer may have to call at the property. If there are no problems with the line connection, again this service is FREE (subject to survey)

- For whatever reason, if any repair work is required to reconnect the telephone line, the engineer will quote a cost before any work is carried out. You can then decide whether you wish to go ahead with the connection based on whether you can afford the required work.

There are also a number of local cable companies who supply telephone services. Charges can vary widely, depending on whether you also rent your cable television services from the same company.

TELEVISION LICENCE
The cost of buying a television licence may seem expensive but just consider the £1,000 fine that is imposed should you get caught watching television without one! You will need a licence if you have a television or a computer that receives television programmes. Application forms are available from any post office or telephone Television Licensing (see Useful Contacts).

Pat's Top Tip
It's worth asking if there is already a valid licence for the property. If the agent or landlord doesn't have this information then contact the National Television Licence Records Office (details from your local post office). You may be able to save a little money if the last tenants did not cancel the existing licence.

OTHER FINANCIAL COMMITMENTS

Do you have regular loan payments to make? What about your travelling costs: train/bus fares, the cost of running your car including tax, insurance, fuel, MOT and maintenance costs?

PERSONAL EXPENSES

Don't forget that you have to eat as well! A regular diet of baked beans on toast can lose its appeal if that's all you can afford.

SOCIAL LIFE

If you rent this property can you still afford to have fun? You may be used to going out with your friends several times a week, having take-away food whenever you fancy or going on holiday now and again. How will you feel if you suddenly can't afford your usual lifestyle because all your spare cash is needed to pay the bills?

Tenants can run into financial trouble simply because they did not do their sums at the start. Just living your life normally incurs a lot of expense. Make sure that you can pay the rent regularly and cover everything else too. It's not a good plan to rent a lovely property if you can't afford to live as well.

The best way to find out what you can afford is to sit down for a few minutes with a pen and paper to work out your budget. On a sheet of A4 paper make two columns, one on the left and one of the right. Write down in one column exactly what your total income is (remember to use your net income with tax and other expenses deducted); and then in another column write down all your projected expenses, this should include all the items mentioned previously plus anything else you can think of. If you take your total expenses from your income what does that leave you? Is it enough to survive on?

With an annual net salary of £15,000, your budget sheet could look like this:

Item	Monthly Income	Monthly Expense
Wages	£1,250	
Rent payable		£500
Gas charges		£20
Electricity charges		£20
Water charges		£15
Council tax		£75
Credit card payment		£50
Food		£200
Car expenses		£200
TOTAL	**£1,250**	**£1,080**

Amount left over after expenses = £170.

As you can see, even on an annual net salary of £15,000 there is not much room for wild parties or too many nights out with your friends. I hope this shows the need for careful planning before starting on the road to renting – especially if you are going it alone.

2

FINDING THE RIGHT PROPERTY

You will find properties for rent advertised everywhere, including local newspapers, specialist companies on the high street such as residential letting agents and on the Internet. You will quickly realise that there are hundreds of properties available at any given time; the trick is to find quickly exactly what you are looking for in the location you need and at a price to suit your budget. The time of year to look is also important as there are good periods and very bad periods in the rental market.

The busiest time of the year for all types of lettings is usually June, July and August. For student rentals the busy patterns follow the university terms. This means that empty properties for rent will become harder to find just before the start of each term: Easter, Summer and Christmas. Naturally, the best properties get booked first and the nearer you get to the start of the university term, the higher the prices could be. The worst period for letting agents – and therefore the best for prospective tenants – is usually during January and February. This is a very quiet time with not much movement in the business of lettings, people will have organised their housing requirements before Christmas and letting agents will be twiddling their thumbs until Easter. Now could be a good time to make an offer on a property you have your eye on, landlords will not want their investment sitting empty and will probably be willing to negotiate on the monthly rental charges. During the first two months of the year there could be some real bargains to be had.

Starting Your Search
When to Look
Ideally, you should start looking 4–6 weeks before you plan to move in. Usually landlords will not hold a property empty for longer than this as they won't risk losing rental income. You may be asked to start your tenancy earlier than you really need to if you begin your search too early, which means having to pay rent for an extra week or two to make sure that a particular property is secured. Try to work out exactly what you are looking for, the size and price of the property and the area that you prefer. If you have a clear idea about your requirements you will not waste any of your own time or that of the letting agent/ landlord.

Where to Look
There are many different methods of finding a property, and each method has its own benefits and risks. One of the following is sure to be the right one for you:

LOCAL PROPERTY PAPERS
Properties for rent are advertised in just about every local newspaper. Many newspapers will carry a free property supplement where you will find not only all the major local letting agents and the properties that they have to offer but also a large number of private adverts where landlords can advertise their own properties for rent.

Local newspapers are a great place to check out what's available and you can take your time to compare prices of similar properties with several different agents or private landlords. As you are reading the information on your own or with friends you will not have the problem of being hassled by enthusiastic agents (or landlords) into making a quick decision – one which you may regret at a later date.

If you see a property you like you will have time to do some research on the local area before you make the appointment to view.

INTERNET
If you have access to the Internet – and most people do – you will probably already know that this is a valuable resource. Details of thousands of letting agents and their properties to let, locally, nationally and even internationally, are available for your inspection at the click of a mouse. If you consult any of the major search engines – Google, Ask Jeeves, Lycos, Yahoo, Excite, etc., about letting agents in the particular area you require, you will be offered a mine of information to sift through. Most Internet-wise agents will be able to offer a virtual tour of their properties; this way you can look through the interior of any house on their website without the bother of arranging a viewing until you see something you really like.

LOCAL LETTING AGENTS
When looking for letting agents, always ensure that they are members of one of the regulatory bodies like ARLA (Association of Residential Letting Agents), NALS (National Approved Letting Scheme) or NAEA (National Association of Estate Agents). Before agents are accepted as members of any of these industry associations, they will have to be seen to be conducting their business to certain high standards. The largest association for letting agents is ARLA whose code of practice demands that a member agent should:

● Hold professional indemnity insurance, separate client accounts and a client money-bonding scheme, and employ trained, qualified staff

● Demonstrate a comprehensive understanding of the

regulations, obligations and legalities that apply to landlords, tenants and agents

- Have access to a complaints process over the service standards of letting agents and to procedures for resolving disputes over deposits between landlords and tenants.

The other main benefit of using letting agents to help you find your property is that:

- They will have a large choice of property in the area you need

- They will have good local knowledge

- They will be able to give you full details and answer any questions you may have about their properties

- They will also have to ensure, by law, that the property is in a safe condition and has undergone all the necessary gas and electric safety checks required under the current legislation for rented property.

RELOCATION AGENTS

Relocation companies are normally used by companies and individuals who have exact requirements regarding the type of property and the area that is needed but no time to make the search for themselves. You will find details of these companies on the Internet (Association of Relocation Agents) or in your local *Yellow Pages* directory. These agents will do all the leg-work; they will ring letting agencies and vet many properties on your behalf until they find around half a dozen that match your requirements. Relocation agents will collect their client, take them to view all the prospective properties, do all negotiations on their behalf, assist with the check-in at the start and check-out at the end of the tenancy. Sounds perfect

Pat's Top Tip

If an agent doesn't have a suitable property on the day, you can call him and ask that he telephone you when something suitable comes along or to be put on the mailing list. However, agents have very short memories. They may call you once or even twice but if you are really keen to find a property, you need to telephone them every week; this will let them know that you are a serious prospective tenant. If you simply wait for them to call, you could miss out and, if they have tried to contact you without success, they will file your details in the back of their drawer or in the waste bin.

doesn't it? There is a snag, however, their fees are usually very high and you will have to pay not only the relocation agent but the letting agent's normal fees as well. These companies provide a very useful service when time and effort is a bigger issue than money.

Notes for Students

Talk to your Student Union Advice Centre or University Accommodation Office. They will have a list of approved properties and landlords. Letting agents are reluctant to consider renting property to students so inside information is vital. Often other students will have experience of local properties, good and bad, and can report back to the SU to warn others – or even to recommend!

Things to Consider
When looking for somewhere you are about to spend at least the next six months of your life you should ask yourself the following questions:

Transport
Where are you working or studying? How easy will it be to get there? If you drive, what are the local roads like during the rush hour or, if you travel by public transport, how reliable is it at the time you wish to travel?

Location
If you don't know the area well, you should take a good look around on more than one occasion. When you visit a property it may be during the evening; try going back for a look around over the weekend or during the daytime to get a complete picture of the area and the people. A road that looks quite civilised during the day can become a popular and noisy party spot on a Saturday night.

Entertainment
What facilities are available that are easy to reach? Look at the things that make you happy in life: your hobbies, how you spend your spare time. How close or conveniently sited are local sports clubs, leisure centres, pubs, restaurants and shopping facilities? Think about your lifestyle and your needs and make sure that the property is in the right location to allow you to enjoy them.

Money
Can you afford the rent? If you have done your sums, as mentioned in the previous chapter, you will know how much you can afford. If you are thinking about renting an unfurnished property remember to factor in the cost of furniture and other essentials. Unless you can beg or borrow most of what you need, you will have to buy a host of kitchen equipment as well as beds, wardrobes, chairs and maybe even curtains if they are not supplied. Larger

items need to be ordered several weeks in advance if you are buying from new – or you could start your life in your new home by using the floor to sit or sleep on. Or, as I did once many years ago, you could always borrow a set of garden furniture until your delivery arrives. You would be amazed at how many things you can do with a patio table and chairs or the odd sunbed. All your sitting, sleeping and dining problems solved at a stroke – and quite comfortable once you get used to it. My family and I lived like this for several months when we moved to a new house and deliveries were much later than promised. I discovered that Christmas dinner tastes just as good whether eaten at a posh dining table or the plastic wobbly kind!

It's surprising how many household items you can do without if you really have to. If there is a cooker with a grill then you don't necessarily need a toaster, a microwave, a deep fat fryer or a sandwich toaster – the list is endless. It's great, of course, to have all those handy gadgets if you can afford to but not the end of the world if you can't. Provided you do the washing-up frequently you won't need a full set of cutlery or china. Just two sets of bed linen are needed: one on and one in the wash! If you really think about it we all have far too many of everything and could, if necessary, manage without most of the clutter that surrounds us – thus saving a lot of money from the start.

Pat's Top Tip

Most rental prices are negotiable. If you think a property is just perfect for you it's always worth offering a little lower than the stated price. Don't be silly about it, of course. For example, if a property is advertised for £625 per calendar month, try offering £600. Over the course of a 12-month tenancy you will have saved yourself £300.

No matter which method you have chosen for finding your property, you will either end up dealing directly with the landlord of the property, or dealing with the letting agent whom the landlord has instructed to manage the property.

Dealing with Letting Agents
No letting agent can lawfully charge a fee to register you or to provide you with information about a property to rent. If any agent tries to get money from you when you first walk in the door, leave fast and try somewhere else. The time to hand over money will only be when you have found a property that you are interested in. It is at this stage that the agent will ask for a holding deposit, which will cover his administration charges – the work needed to begin checking your references. Sometimes part of this fee is offset against charges to you at a later date. If there are problems with your references or you pull out of the deal at the last minute, then you will lose your holding deposit. So be very sure that you have chosen your new home wisely before putting your money down.

If you have a bad credit history or have had any County Court judgments made against you that are still in force, you need to inform the letting agent. They will usually check you out with a credit reference agency so your credit history will not remain a secret for long. It is better for you to be honest with them from the start. If you are unfortunate enough to be in this difficult financial position, you will undoubtedly need to pay either your first six months' rent in advance or to have a guarantor – this is someone who needs to sign the tenancy agreement and will take responsibility for guaranteeing that the landlord will receive the rental payments. The agent will need to take up references on the guarantor also. If you default with your payments at any time this guarantor will be hounded for any outstanding monies. It is for this reason that guarantors, unless they happen to be your parents, are very hard to find!

Dealing with Landlords

A holding deposit may be requested. This should not exceed the equivalent of around two weeks' rent. It shows that you are serious in your intention to rent the property and gives the landlord reassurance. However, when paying money in advance to someone you don't know, it's a good idea to take a few sensible precautions. Always get firm contact details of your prospective landlord including his home address and home telephone number together with a mobile number.

Always get a signed receipt and a guarantee in writing that this deposit will be refunded or deducted from your initial payments. Do not pay any rent or large security deposit in advance to a private individual. These monies are not due for payment until the landlord actually hands over the keys on the day you move into the property. If the landlord gets his hands on your money in advance, there is sometimes a danger that you will not only lose the property but you will lose your money into the bargain.

Don't take a risk. The landlord may come across as a friendly and helpful person but things can still go wrong. There are many published stories of hapless tenants (usually students as they tend to be young and the landlord thinks they won't fight back later) who have foolishly paid large sums up front, well in advance of the moving-in date. Then they find later that the landlord has rented the property to someone else or has only given them a mobile telephone number as a contact point, and has suddenly disappeared without trace with their money.

Multiple Occupancy

This simply means any property that is split into separate flats or bedsits that are not occupied by members of the same family and which, mostly, will have communal areas like the kitchen or bathroom or shared stairways. Lots of student accommodation can be termed as HMOs (Houses with Multiple Occupancy); this description is also applied to guest houses or bed-and-breakfasts, hostels and refuges. There are strict regulations regarding these kinds of properties. Their owners will need to register with the local authority who try to ensure that all rules concerning health and safety are adhered to. These regulations cover the landlord's responsibilities regarding maintenance of the building and its contents, the supply of basic services like gas, electricity and water, and general health and safety issues. Rules can vary from one authority to another so you will need to check the registration details locally of any particular property.

Becoming a Lodger

An easy option for any house owner who has a spare room is to rent it out and earn some extra cash. Owners are allowed to earn a certain amount every year from taking in lodgers without having this income taxed by the Inland Revenue. Being a 'lodger' in someone else's house means sharing the other facilities with the owner, such as the kitchen and the bathroom. The only space that you can really call your own will be the bedroom you are actually renting – and even this won't be totally private if the owner has his own key to your door.

As a 'lodger' you will have fewer rights, legally, than for other types of tenancies. These kinds of rental arrangements are usually very relaxed but the house owner's responsibility regarding health and safety issues is the same and it is worth insisting on a written agreement of some kind, however informal, although this cannot, of course, be a standard assured shorthold agreement. Ask your landlord to put in writing the general rules and regulations of renting your room and any special conditions that concern the communal areas. Also, make sure this agreement states how much the rent is to be, when/ how often it is to be paid, the amount of any security deposit you have to pay to the landlord, and how much notice to leave the property you and your landlord need to give each other. Notice for lodgers is usually as short as one week and there are no legal requirements for a mini-mum notice period either way, it is normally just down to a polite agreement between both parties. Other things to find out are:

- What is included in the rent? Usually gas, electricity, water charges and council tax are paid by the land-lord and should be included – but make sure you check

- Would it be a problem if you have a friend to stay over once in a while?

- What are the other lodgers like, if there are any? It is important to meet them – and for them to meet you, to make sure you are happy with the other people you will be sharing your living space with

- Is there an inventory of contents? Although you are only renting a room, it is still important to have a record of the condition of the decoration and all the contents. You will have paid a security deposit and although this will be smaller than when renting a flat or house, this money still needs to be protected.

About You

No matter whom you deal with, now is the time that the agent or landlord will be wanting to know more about you and your personal circumstances. When dealing with a landlord, this process will most likely be very informal but when dealing with a letting agent, you and your fellow tenants will need to complete an application form.

The following information will be required:

- Your personal details

- Current employer and salary

- Details of referees – normally employer, previous landlord, bank or even a personal referee

- Details of your guarantor – if your salary is not enough to cover the rent or you have a troubled credit history, the agent will ask for someone to guarantee the rent. He will need to take up references on the guarantor who will be taking full responsibility for the rental payments during the tenancy. If you cannot pay the rent for any reason your guarantor will be contacted and any outstanding rent demanded.

Are You a Suitable Tenant?
References
The agent or landlord will write to the people you have named, so it is polite to let your referees know this beforehand. Make sure that all the people named are happy to give you a good reference; if any refuse or give a negative reference you will undoubtedly lose your holding deposit.

Restrictions
You will also be asked if you smoke, have any pets or children, and for how long you wish to rent. Many landlords have restrictions on the kind of tenants they are looking for. If you are a heavy smoker, have three dogs and a cat plus a couple of children, the sad fact is that you could find yourself with little choice when looking for a property to rent.

Information Point
If you are blind or deaf it is unlawful for a landlord to place restrictions on a guide dog or a hearing dog.

Here is an example of the kind of application form currently in use by letting agents.

TENANT'S APPLICATION

WARNING: if a false statement is made knowingly or recklessly on this form by or at the instigation of the proposed tenant the Landlord will be entitled to terminate the tenancy under Ground 17 in the Housing Act

YOUR NAME, CURRENT ADDRESS AND PERSONAL DETAILS

Mr Mrs Miss Ms Other	Last name
Forenames (list all)	
House	
Place	
Town	
County	
Postcode	
Length of time at this address (years/months) *(if under 3 yrs give previous addresses overleaf)*	
Status: Owner　　　Council Tenant　　　Private Tenant　　　Living with parents/friends	
Do you have any adverse credit history or CCJ's against you? Yes　　No *(this includes bankruptcy etc) (if yes give details overleaf)*	
Are you entitled to any form of diplomatic privilege in the UK? Yes　　No *(if yes give details overleaf)*	
Tel no (home)	
Tel no (work)	
Mobile no	
Fax no	
Email address	

Status: Married   Single   Divorced   Separated   Widowed   Living together
Date of birth
National Insurance no
Nationality

YOUR EMPLOYER (IF APPROPRIATE)

Contact name/position	
Employer's name	
Address	
Employer's tel no	Employer's fax no
Position held	Payroll/service/pension no
Gross salary/pension pa	
Status: Employed Self-employed On contract Retired Unemployed Student	
Commencement date with this employer *(note: if less than 18 months provide previous employers and dates)*	
Will your employment change before the proposed tenancy starts?	

YOUR LANDLORD (IF APPROPRIATE)

Name
Address
Landlord's tel no
Type of tenancy

Reason for leaving
Monthly rent
Date tenancy commenced
Date tenancy terminates (eg if you have to give notice)

BANK/BUILDING SOCIETY DETAILS (CURRENT A/C ONLY)

Bank
Address
Tel no
Account name
Sort code
Account no

PERSONAL REFERENCE

Full name
Address
Tel no
Relationship
How long has this person known you?

OTHER INFORMATION

Do you smoke? *(if yes say how many per day)*
Names and ages of children living with you *(give details overleaf if not enough space)*
Do you have any pets? *(if yes give details)*

If you ask any letting agent who their perfect tenant would be, their answer will usually be someone who is single, professional and a non-smoker. Tenants (and tenancies) of this description are usually the easiest to manage from start to finish and will cause fewer problems from the agent's point of view.

When you are searching for somewhere to rent you can use the services of as many letting agents as you wish and there should, in theory, be no limit to the number of properties you can view to enable you to find just the right one.

Make sure you stick to your budget, agents will always try to offer you more expensive properties just on the off-chance that you will succumb to temptation. An extra £50 per month may not sound a lot but this sum could cover part of your council tax or your electricity bill and the extra expense may mean that you won't be able to afford something else you need.

Viewing Properties
The letting agents will earn a lot of commission from your tenancy (on a 6-month tenancy at £600 per month, the agents will earn £500-£700). Make sure that they earn it. They should be happy to let you view as many properties as you wish to ensure that you rent your new home through them.

Experience shows, though, that the more places you see the more confused you will get. By the time you have seen your fifth or sixth property you will have forgotten what the first one was like. So try to discriminate, know exactly what you are looking for at the start, what facilities you need in your ideal property and where you would like to be. Check out the area so you know which parts of town are not worth looking at.

Things to Remember
Be considerate: If there are tenants already living in the property you want to view, don't try to book viewings late

at night or early in the morning. 'Do as you would be done by' – remember that when you are in their position at the end of your tenancy you will also expect consideration.

Having said that, do not let a current tenant put you off from having a good look round. It often feels more intrusive if a property is full of someone else's personal things. You have to treat the whole process in a business-like manner. You need to know what things belong to the tenant and what will stay in the property.

How Does the Property Look?
CLEANLINESS
If a property is in a dirty state when you are viewing it, it could be unlikely to improve very much by the time you move in, in spite of reassurances to the contrary. There are degrees of cleanliness; if the place is just a bit neglected and dusty this shouldn't present too much of a problem. However, if there is ingrained dirt everywhere and stains all over the carpets then living in this state could be unpleasant. The agent or landlord will usually say that the property will be cleaned or sometimes redecorated when the current tenants vacate. If this doesn't happen, and sadly this is sometimes the case, can you easily rectify the situation with a little elbow grease or will you have to live with the place in this condition?

SIGNS OF NEGLECT
If there is evidence of un-repaired damage – leaking gutters, flaking exterior paintwork – this may tell you that the landlord is uncooperative or unwilling to pay any money to keep up with the general maintenance of the property. When you are inside take a look at the following:

CEILINGS
Are there any water stains present? Are the light fittings in good condition? What about signs of damp or black mould speckles above the shower or bath?

WALLS
Is the decoration in a tired/poor condition? Are the electrical sockets in good condition?

WINDOWS
Are any broken? Is there heavy condensation? Are all the fittings complete? Are there any window locks? Can you see any signs of damp around the window frame or on the walls closest to the window?

FLOORING
Is the floor covering in good condition? Are there any holes or loose floorboards? Are the rugs hiding any major damage or staining?

APPLIANCES AND FURNITURE
Once you have found out what is staying, pay attention to how old things look. Do the seats on the sofa sag due to broken springs? Do the plugs look safe? Are the dining table and chairs in a stable condition?

GARDEN
Is it currently running wild? Are the fences in good repair?

GARAGE
Is it secure and the lock in good order? Are you allowed to use it or does the landlord use it for his or her own storage? Is it watertight? Look inside for signs of damage to the roofing or for wet areas on the walls or floor.

Don't be afraid to ask questions – a shower that has leaked once may still have a problem which could cause you inconvenience during your own tenancy. It's worth reminding the landlord that it is in his own best interests to present the property in a good condition, because as a tenant you are required to return the property in the same condition at the end of your tenancy.

SIGNS OF DAMP

Sometimes you can tell if a property has any kind of damp problem by a musty smell that hangs about the place, especially if the house has been empty for a while. Even if you can't detect any kind of aroma look for signs of mould. Take a look into corners and behind furniture. Mould marks are difficult to remove and you may see ingrained black staining to walls, skirting boards, around windows or ceilings, where someone has attempted to clean the marks off.

If you rent a property that has a damp problem, you are expected to make all efforts to keep the problem to a minimum by using any extractor/ventilation fans that are fitted and by opening windows to allow air to circulate freely wherever there are problem areas. Even if the landlord has provided you with a de-humidifier unit, if you haven't managed to keep the effects of the problem controlled then you could have money taken out of your *Security Deposit* for the extra cleaning or redecorating; it may be concluded that the problem has been made worse by your neglect during the tenancy. This sounds unfair but, unfortunately, tenants are penalised financially for this problem all the time.

Damp and/or serious condensation is not pleasant to live with and is not good for your health so picking up these signs when you're viewing a property is much more helpful than finding out about them after you have moved in and are paying the rent.

STORAGE SPACE

Is there any? It's amazing how many personal bits and pieces one person can collect. Are there enough cupboards or bookcases for your requirements? Where can you put your computer? Are there sheds or a garage that you can use for storage? What about the loft? Has the landlord locked off any rooms to use for his own storage?

Pat's Top Tip

When you first step into a property stand still for a few seconds and use all your senses. Breathe in, what can you smell? What do you feel? Does the property smell clean? Warm? Musty? Damp? Is there any kind of animal smell? Can you hear nearby traffic or sounds from the neighbours' houses? Are there any serious draughts?

FITTINGS

Are there enough electrical sockets? Are the light switches conveniently placed? Do the electrics look in disrepair? Are there any bare wires showing? Do all the lights work?

Remember: If the property is in need of cleaning or the garden is very overgrown, the agent or landlord may promise that work will be carried out before you move in. It is always a good idea to get any promises confirmed in writing as once you have paid your deposit, things sometimes get overlooked or landlords and agents suddenly suffer from amnesia and can't remember what was agreed verbally. Once you have moved into the property, your bargaining position is weakened as you have already signed the agreement which states that you are accepting the property as seen.

Information Point

When you move out, if you have left the property in a dirty condition or the garden untidy, then you will be heavily penalised. Try to make sure that these things are in a good condition from the beginning, before you take on the tenancy.

UNWANTED VISITORS

What about signs of insect infestation? Many properties suffer from unwanted visitors such as mice – don't be afraid to take a peek into cupboards and corners when viewing. Look for signs of 'droppings' or in older houses there may be woodworm present. Whilst this is primarily a problem for the landlord it's quite likely that any furniture that you place in the property will become infected and damaged too. If you should then take that furniture into a house that you buy some time in the future, there is a real risk that the woodworm could damage your own property.

And then there's the problem of *fleas*...

Pat's Top Tip

Has any previous tenant owned a cat or dog? Telltale signs can be 'fluffing' or thread pulls to corners of carpets or furniture, or pet hairs on the linings of curtains. A quick check during your viewing will tell you what you need to know. Flea eggs can lie dormant in carpets or other soft furnishings for months and it can be a nasty surprise suddenly to find yourself in the middle of an itching epidemic when they wake up and start feasting on you.

I have visited many empty properties over the years, both new and old buildings, to carry out inspections and suddenly felt that familiar 'tickling' sensation as the tiny inhabitants sense a warm body to feed on and start climbing up my ankles. One house was so heavily infested that I found the only way to monitor how many were actually trying to feed off me was to remove my jeans and stand in the bath! It was the safest place to stand in a very lively house. The letting agent was immediately informed

Notes for Students

According to the National Union of Students around 16 per cent of UK students live in properties that have vermin infestations of some kind or another. Mostly students will be dealing directly with a landlord, this means that sometimes the standard of the property available may not be quite so good. Landlords do not have to be members of any professional body, or have a business reputation to protect, so some seem to feel that they can offer a property for rent in any condition they please. Don't be fobbed off, there are some unscrupulous landlords out there who are happy to rent to students but who will not supply their property or its contents in a good or even safe condition; they are also more likely to try and ignore health and safety issues.

but could not arrange for fumigation until the next day. In the meantime the new tenants arrived with their baby daughter – and their van full of furniture. I dispatched the husband to the local pet shop to buy as many cans of flea spray as he could afford! With a quick bit of work we managed to solve the immediate problem and make the house safer (and less itchy), before the removal men unloaded.

TAKE YOUR TIME

It's almost unbelievable but most tenants will only spend a few short minutes looking round when choosing a new place to live and can be disappointed with the general condition of the property when they arrive on moving-in day. Take your time, arrange a second or even a third viewing if you wish to make sure that you are happy. Both letting agents and landlords will try to put a little pressure on you for a decision, sometimes saying that they have other people who are interested in renting the property. Always be polite but don't on any account let yourself be rushed into making the wrong decision.

Health and Safety Checks
Carbon Monoxide
It is a worrying fact that every year at least 30 people die and illness and injury are caused to thousands more from the effects of carbon monoxide poisoning caused by gas appliances that have not been correctly fitted or serviced, unsafe appliances and house fires. Carbon monoxide is invisible and has no smell – and it can kill. It is a legal duty for all landlords to provide a safe environment for their tenants. If they fail to do this there are stiff penalties – heavy fines and even imprisonment plus, of course, they are liable for payment of damages to any tenant who is injured due to their neglect. Small carbon monoxide detectors are readily available (some just the size of a credit card) and, while not a legal requirement, they can give a useful warning when problems occur.

Gas
If there are any gas appliances ask to see the Gas Safety Certificate. It is a legal requirement, since Gas Safety Regulations came into force in 1994, for any rental property with a gas supply to have a current Safety Certificate to state that all gas appliances have been checked and passed as safe by a Corgi Registered professional who is qualified to carry out this kind of work. This safety check should be carried out annually and applies to appliances and equipment fitted both to the mains gas supply and to liquid, propane or Calor gas. A copy of the Safety Certificate should be available in the property or given to the tenants for their records. If any pipework or appliance is found to be in a dangerous or defective condition it must be repaired or replaced as soon as possible.

Information Point

It is the legal responsibility (*under Regulation 35(2) of the 1994 Gas Safety Act*) of the owner of any gas appliance and pipework to ensure that it is maintained in a safe condition so as to prevent risk of injury to any person.

During the check all the following will be inspected:

- Escape of gas or any dangerous fumes

- Operating pressures

- Flame combustion

- Heat output

- Adequate ventilation and flues

- Any other obvious defects.

An annual service check is not the same as the safety inspection because the normal service procedure is not detailed enough to comply with the safety regulations, so even if the landlord tells you that he has the boiler serviced every year you should still insist on seeing the Safety Certificate.

Solid Fuel/Oil

If the property has solid fuel or oil-fired heating systems then the landlord also has a duty to make sure that these are regularly maintained and that there are adequate ventilation systems and flues.

Here is a sample Gas Safety Certificate:

LANDLORD'S GAS SAFETY RECORD

This inspection is for gas safety purposes only to comply with the Gas Safety (Installation and Use) Regulations. Flues have been inspected visually and checked for satisfactory evacuation of products of combustion. A detailed internal inspection of the flue integrity, construction and lining has NOT been carried out.

Inspecting Installer (Name of Corgi Registered Gas Engineer/ Company) ....

Corgi Registration No ....

Address ....

....

Telephone Number ....

INSPECTION ADDRESS: LANDLORD'S NAME & ADDRESS:

....

....

Tenant's Name: Present? Yes/No

APPLIANCE DETAILS

Location   Make   Model   Type

Flue   Op.Pressure/Smoke Match

INSPECTION DETAILS

Satisfactory Termination   Visual Condition

Adequate Ventilation   Safe to Use?

DETAILS OF ALL FAULTS & RECTIFICATION WORK REQUIRED

Warning notice issued/Warning sticker

Number of Appliances Tested .... Signed .... Date ....

Received on behalf of Landlord/Tenant/Agent ....

Electrical Appliances

Most letting agents now insist that landlords have an annual electrical safety inspection certificate to ensure that all the appliances and wiring are in a good condition. The latest government rules regarding electrical safety state that any **new** installations must be carried out by a 'registered competent person' who can issue a 'Part P Certificate' to state that the works comply with BS 7671. This document should be left in the property along with the gas safety certificate.

In any case, whether renting through an agent or directly with your landlord, he has a legal responsibility to ensure that all appliances are in a safe condition. Things to look out for when you are viewing a property are:

- Scorched or damaged electrical sockets

- Cracked or old looking plugs

- Exposed wiring

- Damaged or frayed insulation.

Smoke Alarms

If a property has been built since June 1992 you would expect there to be a mains-operated smoke detector to protect each floor. There is no legal requirement, at the time of writing, that smoke alarms be fitted in a rented property that was built before 1992 but they can be life-savers and are recommended by the Fire & Safety Officers' Association. If there are none fitted in your new rented home, ask your landlord to fit a cheap, battery-operated one or however many are appropriate to the size of the property. It is recommended that a smoke alarm be fitted on the stairway and in the hall of each floor of the property. As a last resort you can always buy one yourself and place it where it will be of most help to give a warning should there be a fire. If you do choose to fit one yourself, remember to ask your landlord for permission as any screw holes you make will need to be made good at the end of your tenancy.

Furnishings
There are now also many regulations covering tenant safety with regard to furniture and equipment. It is, therefore, a growing trend for landlords to supply properties in an unfurnished state (however, research shows that there is little, if any, price difference between the cost of renting an empty property and renting a fully furnished one).

Information Point

If the property is furnished check the chairs, beds and other soft furnishings for fire safety labels. It is illegal to furnish a rented property with upholstered items that do not comply with fire regulations.

These regulations are many and a copy of the Guide to the Furniture and Furnishings (Fire) (Safety) Regulations can be obtained from the Internet or by writing to The Consumer Safety Unit at the Department of Trade & Industry (see Useful Contacts on page 150).

Briefly, under the Consumer Protection Act 1988 Section 12(1), it is an offence for any landlord to supply furniture, upholstery and upholstered furnishings, loose fittings or permanent or loose covers to which the regulations apply, unless they meet what is known as the 'cigarette or match test'.

You can check compliance by looking for a label, usually under seat cushions; it should state that the covers and fillings are made of fire resistant material and will pass the 'match flame' and 'smouldering cigarette' resistance tests. Most items of furniture manufactured here in the UK after 1990 should be of sufficient quality to meet the necessary standards and will have the label present – unless some helpful person has cut it off to make things look tidy (as has happened in countless cases). Any item in a rented property that does not comply with the regulations must be removed before the letting. If the landlord leaves dangerous items in the property during the tenancy and there is a fire, he will be liable to prosecution. This offence carries a punishment of six months' imprisonment or a maximum fine of £5,000 (or both).

Items covered by the regulations are:

- Beds, padded headboards, mattresses and pillows

- Three-piece suites, armchairs and sofas

- Futons, sofa beds

- Loose covers for any upholstered item

- Scatter cushions, seat pads and bean bags

- Garden furniture suitable for indoor use and nursery furniture.

There are several exempt items that do not have to comply with the regulations. These include antique furniture or anything made before 1950, bed linen, duvets, pillowcases, carpets and curtains and loose covers for mattresses.

Furnished or Unfurnished – What to Expect
Furnished

The following is a list of the minimum recommended contents for a furnished property, these items are not a legal requirement and will vary from landlord to landlord but in general you could expect the following:

KITCHEN
Cooker, washing machine, refrigerator, dinner/tea service for 4–6 people, set of saucepans, frying pan, set of cutlery, kettle, vacuum cleaner, set of glassware, small number of kitchen utensils, iron and ironing board, dustpan and brush. (Optional: freezer, tumble dryer.)

LIVING ROOM
Settee and armchairs, coffee table or small side table, bookshelf/sideboard or similar storage space.

DINING ROOM
Dining table with 4/6 chairs as appropriate, sideboard or similar storage space.

BEDROOM
Double bed if in main bedroom, otherwise single bed (and mattress), appropriate hanging space, chest of drawers, bedside table, table lamp.

OUTSIDE
Dustbin, television aerial.

GARDEN
Should be left in a tidy condition with a working lawn mower and some basic tools to enable the tenant to maintain the garden, unless a gardener is provided.

However, it is not unusual for the landlord not to leave such basics as a mower but you are still expected to keep any grass in a tidy condition.

Take your time when assessing the above items; if there is any basic piece of equipment missing, now is the time to request that the landlord provides it. Equally, if there are any items in the property that you don't need, the landlord may be able to remove them before you move in. Always get any agreements made in writing. After you have signed the tenancy agreement it may be too late, the landlord or his agent is under no obligation to consider any of your requests at this late stage as you have taken the property as seen.

Some items may have been left in the property because the landlord has no room to store them elsewhere and if they are in an old condition, the landlord may not replace or repair them should they break down.

Unfurnished
In an unfurnished property the landlord has no obligation to supply any equipment at all. Most though will supply the basic appliances or 'white goods' in the kitchen: cooker, fridge and washing machine. Again this is not a legal requirement so any or all could be found. Carpets and curtains may or may not also be included.

Pat's Top Tip

When viewing any prospective property you should make sure that you check whether all the items you see are to be left for the tenant. It is a common practice for landlords to remove many items, such as television sets, video recorders, stereos, bedding and more, so be clear on what exactly is on offer.

If in doubt, ask to see a copy of the inventory. This will show you the detailed list of all items contained in the property.

Be aware: one of the disadvantages of renting an unfurnished property is that when you move out, you may cause more damage moving your furniture out of the building than you made during your entire tenancy. This damage, whether major chips or just accidental furniture rub-lines, will be charged to you and taken out of your security deposit. It is your responsibility to leave the property as you found it, allowing for a small amount of normal wear and tear. However, one person's idea of wear and tear allowances is very different from another's; there are no hard-and-fast rules so it is always better to be safe than risk losing money at the end of the tenancy.

3

WHAT TO ASK YOUR AGENT OR LANDLORD

So, you have found your ideal property to rent, what happens now? Whether you find your property through a private landlord or a letting agency, your first concern will be, of course, the monthly rental costs. Try some negotiation if you can. Shaving a little off the rent can save you a tidy sum in the long run. The amount of rent, date it is due and how often you need to pay will be stated in the tenancy agreement so this is the first thing you need to sort out.

There are a few other basic questions that you need to ask before you go any further and sign on the dotted line.

Firstly, if you are using a letting agent it's worth knowing that they offer landlords three levels of service when letting a property. For each one the agent will charge the landlord a different percentage rate for commission and each one will have an effect on your tenancy.

The three service levels under which a property is let are:

- Letting Only

- Rent Collect Only

- Fully Managed.

Notes for Students

Now is also the time to discuss the situation of paying rent during your holiday periods if you plan to be away from the property for any length of time – like the summer break for example. Expect to have to pay the full rent; the landlord will not just keep the house empty waiting for you to return. You may be able to negotiate just paying a retainer, usually 50 per cent of the full rent. If you are happy in the property it will be worth the expense to hold the house for when you need to return. This will also need to be incorporated into the tenancy agreement.

If the property is rented on a *Let Only* basis it means that the agent is simply finding the tenant and doing all the relevant paperwork to complete the let. From the day you move in, having handed over your vast sums of money, the letting agent will completely ignore you again until the end of the tenancy. A *Let Only* service is the cheapest option for a landlord. Typically he will pay 5 to 10 per cent of the total rental income to the agent for commission fees. Under this deal it is the landlord who looks after the property during the tenancy, deals with any problems and repairs and makes sure that the rent is paid on time. It could also be the landlord who will hold your security deposit; try to ensure that this money is held by the letting agent instead. On a *Let Only* the landlord could also carry out the check-out inspection at the end of the tenancy instead of a suitably qualified inventory professional.

On a *Rent Collect* deal, the landlord will pay the agent a slightly higher commission rate – typically 10 to 12 per cent. For this service, the agent will find a suitable tenant, provide all the tenancy paperwork and then arrange to collect the rent from you via your bank account, for the duration of the tenancy. This still means, of course, that the landlord is responsible for any maintenance needed during your stay in the property and will generally organise the check-out inspection at the end. Either the landlord or the agent could be holding your security deposit; you should find out where your money will be held before you close the deal.

Fully Managed means exactly that. The agents will find the tenant, collect the rent during the tenancy and chase you if your payment is late. They will organise any repairs that are needed, carry out regular inspections to make sure that everything is in order and they will arrange your check-out inspection at the end of the term. This is usually the best option for tenants while they are renting a property but the most expensive for landlords. Commission rates charged for a full management service would be, typically, 12 to 15 per cent of the total rent paid. The letting agent will normally hold the security deposit.

What Type of Tenancy?
You should make sure that your tenancy will be a standard Assured Shorthold Tenancy. This gives you certain basic rights as a tenant and offers the best protection for both you and the landlord. If you are dealing with a letting agency, especially one that is a member of one of the regulatory bodies within the industry, you will undoubtedly be provided with this type of tenancy agreement.

If you are dealing directly with a landlord he may not have this organised. He may suggest that it is perfectly OK to pay him the rent in cash each week or month but don't be tempted to agree to this kind of arrangement. Mostly private lets are very informal affairs. This may work up to a point but if there are any problems or disputes during the tenancy, or more likely at the end when you are moving out, your rights as a tenant will be unprotected, as will those of the landlord. You should insist on a formal agreement – an Assured Shorthold.

Most of the legal paperwork needed for a safe let is readily available at any large high street stationer's or on various Internet sites and it is well worth investing £10 or so for the protection that these rental legal packs can offer.

How Much Will it Cost? Fees and Deposits

Always find out at the start exactly what fees are involved when using an agency. It is unlawful for prospective tenants to be charged any kind of fee for registering or at any time during their search for property. Remember that letting agents earn their commissions from the landlords on a successful let so it is in their best interests to give you as much help as you need – free of charge until you are ready to agree to take a property. Of course, agents also make a profit from tenants so ask them to supply details, in writing, of all the charges they expect you to pay when taking up a tenancy. Private landlords will not, of course, usually charge administration fees or fees for getting your references – this could save you a couple of hundred pounds.

The Holding Deposit

Once you have found a suitable property all letting agents and most landlords will charge a holding deposit of some kind. This is usually a minimum of £100 plus VAT. This deposit will be deducted from the final amount that you will be paying to the agent when you sign the agreement on moving-in day. However, you will usually find that this deposit will magically disappear in administration and agreement fees.

Letting agencies make charges to the tenant for drawing up all the legal documents associated with your let – at least £100 plus VAT or more (they will usually charge the landlord an agreement fee also!) and for checking your references to ensure that you are financially secure as a prospective tenant. The holding deposit is entirely separate from the security deposit, you will be asked for the security money at a later stage in the proceedings.

What Reference Checks Will be Needed?

A holding deposit ensures that the property will not be offered to anyone else while your references are being checked out. You will be asked on your application form for details of referees. These will normally be your current employer, a past landlord if you have rented before, details of your bank, and sometimes a personal reference will be asked for. Your details will also be checked with a credit reference agency. If you pull out of the deal for any reason or your references are not good enough, the agent has a right to keep the holding deposit against administration fees, for the work already done on your behalf.

On the other hand, if you decide not to take a property because the agent has given you details about that property that are blatant lies and which makes it totally unsuitable, then you are lawfully entitled to a refund of your holding deposit.

If you feel that the holding deposit is excessive it's a good idea to ask exactly what 'services' are covered by this – and ensure that you are provided with them. It is not unusual for agencies, for example, to include items such as 'checking-in' fees and then later, when the finer details are the last thing on your mind, actually not provide the service for which you are paying.

Insurance

Don't cut corners. Whatever else you want to save money on, don't neglect insurance cover. Cases of burglary and theft are increasing daily. Your letting agency or students' advice centre will be able to advise and recommend insurance for your personal effects while you are renting a property. They can also offer cover for any accidental damage that you may make to the landlord's contents. This is a sensible idea and could save you a lot of money later. You would probably be shocked to know just how many tenants accidentally manage to burn holes in the carpet or damage furniture during the course of their tenancy. If this happens to you the cost of replacing the carpet or suite will have to be borne by you, as the tenant, so insurance cover makes good financial sense.

As with any other insurance, it is worth shopping around to ensure that you are not being overcharged for this service. Any insurance broker should be able to come up with a quote for this kind of cover – just check your local *Yellow Pages*. Always ensure that your policy covers accidental damage; if not, it is not worth taking out.

There are several good companies that provide insurance for tenants: Norwich Union, Letsure and HomeLet all offer good insurance cover but they usually only sell through brokers or letting agencies and not direct to the customer. Premiums are priced according to the postcode that you will be living at and the price that you pay for cover can vary as the broker or agency earns commission on each policy that can range from 15 to 25 per cent. As a very rough guide the monthly premiums for cover of £5,000 could cost from around £8.50, depending on where you live. Different postcode areas attract different premiums, based on a complicated table that lists some areas as a higher risk than others. If you are unlucky enough to live in one of these high-risk areas, the premium will be more expensive and sometimes there will be stipulations about the fitting of window locks and additional locks to the exit doors of your property. You may need to check this out with the letting agent or broker. Landlords are normally quite amenable when it comes to protecting their property; they should be happy to supply any of the additional security devices needed – just so long as you don't ask them to install a complete new burglar alarm system!

A good basic policy should cover not only your own personal possessions and household effects, cash and credit cards but should also include any accidental damage caused to your landlord's building or fixtures and fittings.

As with all insurance policies there will be an excess of at least the first £100 for each claim. Make sure that you read and understand the policy wording document; this is the important small print that explains the cover you are buying in full. It is, unfortunately, normal practice within the insurance industry for you to be sold a policy and then the important policy wording will only be sent to you later with the certificate of cover. It is not a legal requirement for insurers to give you all the small print before taking your money. Ask to see the policy wording before you sign to enable you to make sure that it provides a good range of cover.

Standard insurance cover on a tenant's protection insurance will give you a wide range of benefits. Each company may differ slightly but, in general, you could expect the following items covered on your policy should they be affected by theft, fire, explosion, storm, flood, escape of water or collision by aircraft, animals or vehicles:

- Accidental damage to television, video, personal computers and audio equipment

- New-for-old replacement cover on your contents

- Money and credit cards – up to a specified value (usually £100)

- Replacement locks in case your keys are stolen (specified limit)

- A contribution towards the cost of alternative accommodation

- Contents of garage and sheds or outbuildings (£500)

- Fatal accident benefits (£5,000)

- Compensation for spoiled frozen food (£250)

- Replacement cover for stolen bicycles (£200 max)

- Personal liability (usually £1 million).

Cover needed for your landlord's building and contents should provide for accidental damage to pipes and cables, glass, bathroom fittings and furniture.

The Security Deposit

How much is the security deposit? Both agencies and private landlords will usually require this additional money. This deposit can be the equivalent of one week's rent or it can be as much as one and a half months' rent. It is held until the end of the tenancy and the cost of any damage or cleaning charges are deducted before the money is refunded to the outgoing tenants.

Tenancy Deposit Scheme for Regulated Agents (TDSRA)

Twenty per cent of tenants say that their landlord or agent has withheld their deposit without good reason. To combat this, ARLA (Association of Residential Letting Agents) came up with a scheme for tenants to protect their deposits in the event of any end-of-tenancy disputes. This scheme has now been taken over by a company called *The Dispute Service*. This is a non-profitmaking business set up by several of the regulatory bodies of the lettings industry.

Ask your letting agent if he is a regulated ARLA agent and if he is a member of the Deposit Protection Scheme – not all of them are. If he is a member, you know that your money will be in safer hands. Both the tenant and the landlord can refer any end-of-tenancy disputes to an Independent Case Examiner. At the time of the dispute the agent will be asked to transfer your deposit to TDS – even if this doesn't happen and your money is withheld by the agent for any reason, TDS administers an Assurance Fund which enables the Independent Case Examiner to make his adjudication and pay out the deposit where necessary. Once a decision has been reached, the deposit must be returned to the tenant, less any agreed deductions, within a set period of time. This can be as short as ten days if all the evidence and supporting paperwork is in order. For more detailed information about how the scheme works and a list of member agents, check the TDS website – see Useful Contacts for details.

Pat's Top Tip

There is a legal limit that a landlord can charge you for a security deposit, it cannot be more than the equivalent of two months' rent for an unfurnished property and three months' rent for a furnished property.

Ask who is to hold your security deposit. If you are using a letting agency, ensure that the agency holds this money and not the landlord. Always request that the deposit is placed in a high interest account and that you receive all the interest at the end of the tenancy. Some letting agents will make a set-up charge for this service. This helps to ensure that it will then become uneconomical for you to insist on earning interest on your money and the agent will also then be able to avoid the extra work needed to set up a separate account. They will be able to keep your money in their general clients' account (which is required by law) but at least your money is safe and cannot be released to the landlord without your permission. It is not recommended that the landlord of your property hold the deposit himself. Should there be any disputes later, it is far better for this money to be safely held by a regulated agent until all problems are resolved.

It will soon be a 'civil' offence – but not a legal offence – for agents and landlords not to comply with the rules of the Tenancy Deposit Scheme. If the rules are not followed, neither agents nor landlords will be able to serve the section 21 notice to terminate a tenancy; although it will be permissible for deposits to be passed retrospectively to an approved body (such as a bank or insurance company) at which time a section 21 notice can then be served.

What other costs are there to account for? If the property is a flat there may be a cost for a parking permit, a garage, or even for annual service charges. Always ask for details.

How is the rent to be paid? The safest way is for the rent to be paid on a monthly basis by standing order from your bank account. Never pay in cash. If this really can't be avoided, always get a proper receipt from your landlord or agency. If, for any reason, you are asked to pay your rent in cash on a weekly basis, you should expect to be provided with a rent book – this is a legal requirement.

Rent Payments and Reviews

Ask the agent or landlord to confirm that the rent will not be raised during your agreed tenancy term, this should be written into your agreement. The usual practice is for the rent to be reviewed/increased at the end of each term of the tenancy. During an Assured Shorthold Tenancy, this will be for a fixed term of either six or twelve months. The landlord cannot lawfully raise the rent in the middle of your term of tenancy.

Inventory of Contents and Check-in Procedure

Is there a full inventory for the property? For your protection there should be a full list of the furniture, fixtures and fittings with details concerning their condition. This will be very important on both moving-in day and when you move out. More information about this is given in the following sections.

Is there a check-in procedure? An independent person should be available to check through the inventory with you when you move in. This can be the landlord's or agency's representative or an independent inventory company. If this service is not offered for moving-in day, you could suggest that you employ your own so long as their findings will be acceptable to the landlord. If your letting agent cannot recommend an independent inventory clerk, you will find details of independent inventory companies on the Association of Independent Inventory Clerks' website or you can write to them requesting information. For details, please see Useful Contacts.

The AIIC website contains a comprehensive and helpful list of such professionals with their contact details and a little information about each listing. Charges vary enormously so get a quote before you go ahead. For example, you should expect to pay for a two-bedroom, furnished property, around £50-£80. This covers attendance at the property (normally anything up to two hours depending on the length of the inventory) and a professional inspection with written comments.

This money will be well spent as these comments about the condition of the house will be used at the time of moving out and the return of your large security deposit will depend on the written evidence of condition at time of check-in. More information about this procedure and a sample inventory is included in Chapter 5.

4

CLOSING THE DEAL

Once you have paid your deposit, the agency will begin to check out your references and draw up all the legal documents needed to complete your let. The time taken to complete this procedure varies. One letting agency that I deal with on a daily basis can organise a tenancy within twenty-four hours, another always quotes seven days as the normal time needed to organise the paperwork and references. The amount of work required to set up any let is the same; it's just the speed of the organisers that will vary and how quickly all the relevant documents are available. Don't be afraid of hassling your letting agent who will not want to lose your business – or their commission. It may help if you can contact your referees yourself to speed up the process.

One happy day you will receive the call from the agent, everything is complete and you can arrange an appointment to sign all the paperwork and pay your first month's rent and security deposit. The agency will have instructed you, in writing, exactly how much and in what form to pay this money – no personal cheques are acceptable unless they are received by the agent seven days before your moving-in date – this ensures that the cheque has cleared and the money is safe. Normal payment methods on moving-in day are: banker's draft, cash or a cheque issued by a building society.

There are several documents that need to be read and signed. The largest and most important one is:

The Tenancy Agreement
Literally speaking a tenancy agreement is simply a contract, verbal or written, between you and your landlord. A verbal agreement can set out details such as how much rent is to be charged, when it is payable and whether it includes any bills or other service charges. However, verbal agreements are very difficult to enforce because there will not be any actual proof about what has been agreed. By far the best option is to have a written agreement which is signed by both parties – the tenant and the landlord – and is witnessed by a third party who is not involved in the let.

The Assured Shorthold Agreement
Way back in 1988 a new housing act was set up to offer better protection for both parties concerned with the let and the Assured Shorthold Agreement was born. This was pretty revolutionary at the time as no such protection was available prior to 1988. Tenancies covered are usually for a minimum of six months and a maximum of one year, although there can be exceptions to the minimum term, by agreement with your landlord and the letting agent.

This Assured Shorthold Agreement is now the standard document that you will be required to sign when dealing with letting agents and should also be used by landlords when organising their own let. It lists the rules and regulations of the tenancy of any residential property by private individuals and both landlord and tenant must sign this document to certify that they agree to abide by this document. Should either party be in breach of these obligations then there would be grounds to terminate the tenancy.

The Small Print Explained
To make things a little more complicated a tenancy agreement is made up of 'express terms' or rules and 'implied terms'.

- Express terms are what is actually written in the tenancy agreement or rent book if there is one, or what was agreed verbally

- Implied terms are the rights given by law or established by practice and custom.

Let's take a look at a typical Assured Shorthold Tenancy Agreement. When faced with this document it is tempting for a prospective tenant to glance at the seemingly unending wording and go straight to the back page to complete the necessary signature and date.

Make sure you read the agreement thoroughly before you sign.

You are about to commit to paying someone a large amount of your hard-earned money, ensure that there are no hidden clauses and that all details are correct. If you change your mind later, after you have signed, you will be legally liable to pay the rent to the landlord for the whole term of the agreement and can be pursued by the courts if you default.

An example of a typical Assured Shorthold Tenancy Agreement can be found on page 152.

There are certain basic pieces of information that every tenancy agreement must contain, these are:

- The name and address of the landlord

- The date the tenancy is to begin and the date it is to end

- Details of all the people who are to be the tenants

- How much the rent is and when it is due to be paid each month

- How much the security deposit is to be

- How much notice you and your landlord need to give to terminate the tenancy and how soon this can be done.

Implied Terms
These are additional rules not usually given in writing but they are given as law and implied into the tenancy agreement. They will form part of your contract with the landlord without having even been specifically discussed!

- You have a right to live peacefully in the property

- The landlord must maintain the supplies of water, gas, electricity, sanitation, heating and water and keep them in good working order

- The landlord must carry out basic repairs

- You must take proper care of the property and its contents, fixtures and fittings.

These rules are given by law but may vary depending on the type of tenancy you have. If dealing with a private landlord you may be presented with a 'licence to occupy'. This is not an Assured Shorthold Tenancy and will not offer you the same protection. You should consult a qualified adviser – the Citizens Advice Bureau or a solicitor – before you sign.

Responsibilities of Tenant and Landlord
Both you as the tenant(s) and your prospective landlord have certain responsibilities towards the care of the property and its contents during the extent of the tenancy.

Tenant's Responsibilities
These are many and varied and are listed in detail in the agreement, however, some examples are given below:
As a tenant you will be expected to:

- Pay all gas, electricity and/or fuel oil bills – also water if not paid by your landlord – unless any of these are included in your rent and covered by a clause in the agreement

- Purchase the television licence

- Replace tap washers

- Keep drains clear

- Repair broken glass

- Replace light bulbs and fuses

- Keep the garden in a tidy condition – or no worse than at time of moving in

- Keep the premises in good order and condition and to return the property in the same condition when you vacate.

Tenants should not cause any 'annoyance' to neighbours, should not use the premises for any purpose other than residential and should not, of course, sublet any part of the premises – as tempting as this might be when times are hard!

Landlord's Responsibilities
The landlord must, at all times, keep the property in a habitable condition. Should the property no longer be habitable, perhaps because of flooding or subsidence that requires the tenants to move out through no fault of their own, the landlord should refund any rent already paid for this period.

The Importance of the Break Clause
Make sure that your tenancy agreement contains what is known as a *break clause*. If the landlord or letting agent is

trying to tie you in for a one-year tenancy ensure that you are able to give notice of either thirty or sixty days after six months. If this clause is not included and you have to leave the property before the end of the term, for whatever reason, you could be legally liable for the rent until the stated end of the tenancy. If you are only signing a six-month tenancy agreement you will legally be able to give notice at four months – or of course extend for another six months should you and your landlord choose.

If the Property is Mortgaged

If the landlord has a mortgage on the property it is his responsibility to inform the lender (the building society or bank, etc.) that he is letting the property. He will need to have written permission from the lender before taking on tenants. It is a legal requirement that you as a tenant must be aware of the mortgage situation and when you sign the agreement you will be given a 'Grounds 1 and 2 Notice'. Ground 1 just covers possession of the property by the landlord and Ground 2 is concerned with possession by the lender or mortgagee.

It is important that you are aware of the mortgage situation because if the landlord should default on his mortgage payments the building society/lender can repossess the property and you will of course be without a place to live.

Hidden Clauses

Look out for these additional paragraphs; they may be hidden in the body of the agreement or on a separate sheet at the end. These are just extra rules and regulations that a particular landlord may wish to add. Typical extra clauses could include:

Smokers Clause

This could state that no smoking is allowed in the property, or light smoking only, and any damage caused by smoking to furnishings or decoration will have to be made

Here is a sample Grounds 1 and 2 Notice:

GROUNDS 1 AND 2 NOTICE

Property Address ....

Name of Tenants ....

Ground 1: Gives notice that the tenancy is an Assured Shorthold let under the 1988 Housing Act under Ground 1 and that the property has been previously occupied by the landlord as his own or principal dwelling. Possession may be sought under Ground 1 of the Housing Act. The tenancy is for a minimum of six months in accordance with the tenancy agreement let to the tenants named and that they are responsible for all rent payments whether or not they continue to reside in the property until expiry of the agreement.

Ground 2: The property is subject to a mortgage granted before the beginning of the term and:

a) The mortgagee (building society or other loan provider) is entitled to exercise power of sale conferred on him by the mortgagor by Section 101 of the Law of Property Act 1925 and:

b) The mortgagee may require possession of the property for the purpose of disposing of it with vacant possession in exercise of that power.

good at the end of the tenancy at the outgoing tenants' expense. This means that you will be liable for professional cleaning of all furnishings whether or not they smell of cigarette smoke and, of course, any other damage caused like burn holes in carpets and upholstery.

Dishwasher or Water Softener Clause
The landlord may wish to stipulate that if either of these items are present in the property, they must be kept topped up with salt as failure to do this on a regular basis will

bring a build up of limescale and cause damage to the appliance; repairs or even replacement will then be at the tenants' cost.

Pet Clause
Usually no pets will be allowed in the property! If you have had permission for this then undoubtedly this clause will be in your contract. The tenants will have to agree to have all furnishings and carpets professionally cleaned and/or fumigated at the end of the tenancy and will pay for any damage caused by pets. Cats can cause a lot of damage to carpets by tearing at the edges around the door and can claw furniture. Dogs cause a similar amount of damage but have heavier claws that can score doorframes and other woodwork around the house.

Case History

Hamsters seem to be fairly innocent-looking pets, but one tenant, who did not have permission for any pets in the house, no matter how small, allowed his hamster to escape and it wandered the house for several days before being caught. During this time it had chewed through the wires in the landlord's stereo and electric piano and had made a hole in the sofa to pull out the filling, which it then used to make a nest in the back of the piano! The cost to the tenant of repairing this damage was considerable; sometimes the knock-on effects of keeping pets are not as obvious as you may think.

If you suddenly get the urge to buy a cat or dog during your tenancy, *always* check with the landlord or agent first. There may be all sorts of reasons why animals are not allowed apart from the damage aspect. I have managed property for several landlords who cannot have any animal in any house that they may be moving back into at some stage because this would be against their religious practices – so always ask, and get the answer in writing.

Repair of Electrical Items

Sometimes the landlord will leave items such as a television or video recorder in the property (usually because he has nowhere else to put them) and may stipulate that although happy to leave them he will not be responsible for their repair. If you have this clause you may wish to add your own rider that says should these items break down you will also not be liable for their repair and should be able to dispose of them as necessary should you wish.

General Repairs

Whilst the landlord is responsible for keeping the property in a good state of repair, you should check the agreement in case there are any other clauses regarding general repairs. Occasionally strange clauses may be hidden away trying to make the tenant responsible for general maintenance issues that would normally fall to the responsibility of the landlord. This is unusual but not unheard of.

If there are any clauses in the tenancy agreement that you have strong and realistic objections to, it may be possible to have them crossed out of the text. You should discuss this with your agent or landlord. Most of the standard clauses are legal requirements and of necessity will have to be included. However, if there are additional clauses that you feel are unreasonable you are quite at liberty to request their removal. Both you and the landlord should initial each amendment.

5

MOVING-IN DAY

Money Matters
Today's the day. The agent or landlord will have checked out your credit-worthiness and you will be expected to pay the security deposit and the first month's rent either in cash, by banker's draft or a cheque issued by a building society. (A personal cheque is usually not acceptable, as this would take four to five days to clear. If you need to use this method the agent will have to receive your cheque at least seven days before the tenancy to enable him to bank it and be certain that the money has cleared into his own account.) However, anything can happen (and usually does) so it is best to avoid any advance payment of this kind.

Take your time checking through the paperwork before signing anything or handing over your money. Don't be afraid to ask for a translation, in plain English, of any clause that you are not sure of. Letting agents deal with these legal documents every day of their working lives so should know how to explain fully everything on any document they are asking you to sign. It is also the letting agent's job to ensure that you fully understand the commitment you are about to make, but it's not unknown for you to be rushed through everything so you can sign and pay your money to them as quickly as possible. This allows them to get on with the next poor tenant and therefore the next large commission.

Only when you are quite happy that everything is in order should you sign on the dotted line. Always remember that the tenancy agreement is a legally binding document.

Key Problems
Once you have signed all the paperwork you will then be given the keys and any additional instructions and information about the property.

You will need to sign for the number of keys that you are given. Ideally you could expect the following number of keys to be provided depending on the size of the property:

- 1-bedroom property   1 complete set
- 2-bedroom property   2 complete sets
- 3-bedroom property and above   3 complete sets

It is very rare for tenants to be provided with more than three sets of keys for a property; if there are four sharers expect to get an extra set cut at your own expense.

Even the cost of cutting keys is a competitive business. I needed just one copy of a standard mortise-type key recently; there are two different key cutters local to my office and I was quoted £2.50 from a specialist locksmith or £6 from my local branch of a well-known chain of key cutters/shoe repairers. It pays to shop around even for something as simple as this.

There will often be additional keys that are not for the main front or back door, either given to you at the agent's office or left inside the property. These could be for any of the following: windows, garage, shed, gate padlock, communal store cupboard, remote controls for garages and communal car parks, meter cupboard or radiator bleed keys.

Pat's Top Tip

Sometimes the letting agent or landlord will only have one set of keys available no matter what size the property or how many tenants will be moving in. This is either through lack of time and preparation or just laziness on his part. He may expect you simply to pay for additional sets to be cut.

Try suggesting that you will take the time to have an extra set cut (no more than the above recommendations to suit the size of the property) and that you will bring him the receipt to enable him to reimburse you. This usually works a treat and ensures that you get your required number of keys without being out of pocket.

The cost of cutting a normal Yale-type front door key can be around £4; mortise keys (Chubb or Union type) around £7. As you see, the cost can quickly mount up. It is the landlord's responsibility to provide you with the correct number of keys ready for your moving-in day.

Make sure you check that they all actually work in the relevant locks. Occasionally you will be given badly-cut keys or keys that don't appear to fit any lock in the house. You should immediately inform your agent or landlord of this situation, either in person or on the telephone and then confirm the conversation in writing.

If he shows no sign of providing you with correct keys or offering to pay for cutting additional keys then you may, if all else fails, just have to pay to provide them yourself. As it will ultimately be for your convenience and whilst this does not seem fair in terms of extra expense, there are some occasions in life when, if it is in your own best interests in the long run, you will just have to give in and get on with it!

Make sure that you keep all keys safe, whether working or not, until the end of the tenancy. You will be required to return the same number of keys when you move out so don't be tempted to throw any away, even if they don't work.

Case History

A tenant was given two sets of keys for his newly-rented property. Two of the keys were badly cut and did not work. As they were not vital to his living in the house he simply threw them away. At the end of the tenancy he was charged the sum of £10 to cover the cost of replacing these keys, even though they did not work. As he had never complained he could not prove to the agent that he hadn't simply lost them. If a tenant can't return any key for a particular lock the agent is at liberty to change the lock at the tenant's expense to ensure the security of the landlord's property. A lock change will cost around £60.

The Inventory and Check-in Procedure
The inventory of the property is your best protection. Make sure you use it correctly.

When you move in you will be faced with one of the following three situations:

- You will be met at the property by a professional inventory clerk/agent, landlord or landlord's representative

- You will simply be given a copy of the inventory to check through yourself

- You will be given nothing except the keys.

If you are to be offered a 'check-in' procedure this will mean spending an hour or two with an independent inventory clerk, agency representative or your landlord checking through every item listed on the inventory. This is a long and tedious task, usually taking anything up to two hours but don't allow anyone to rush you through it as this is important. A little work now will reap dividends at the end of your tenancy and will help to protect the vast amount of money you have just paid over as a security deposit. Sometimes, even the professionals will seem like they are in a hurry; always remind them that it's your deposit at stake and it is better to be safe than sorry. A badly-checked inventory is as bad as not having checked it in the first place.

What is more likely, though, is that you will be on your own from this point. If you are provided with a full inventory (and no assistance) you should check it through thoroughly, either on your own or with the help of a professional inventory clerk which you can employ yourself (see Chapter 3). Make sure that a full and correct description is noted regarding marks on the walls, carpets, furniture and all fixtures and fittings, also the state of cleanliness of every item. Remember, this document will be used when you move out and could drastically affect the return of your deposit.

Make any comments you feel appropriate on the inventory, sign and date it, *take a copy for yourself*, then send the original back to the agent or landlord; this should be done within the first seven days of your tenancy. Always keep a copy for your records as both agents and landlords can lose documents and you will then have no proof of the condition of the property when you moved in.

Compiling Your Own Inventory
If there is no inventory for your property, beware! This is potentially the most dangerous situation to find

yourself in. For your own protection you will need to remedy this problem yourself. No inventory means that there is no documentary evidence of the condition of the property on the day you moved in. A relaxed landlord does not always remain that way when you move out. A landlord's memory is a strange thing; he may remember the house being in a much better condition than it actually was, even small areas of damage are forgotten several months or years down the line and you could suddenly find you are charged for damage and cleaning that are not your responsibility. With no proof of the condition of the place when you moved in you are on shaky ground.

Again, if you have learned from previous chapters in this book, you should know well before you move in whether or not there is an inventory for the property. If there is not, try insisting that the landlord employs an inventory clerk to provide one. If he refuses on grounds of cost, you could point out that it is in his own best interest and will protect his investment. If this suggestion doesn't work then, as a last resort, you can always provide your own inventory list or schedule of condition and take photographs of any areas of serious damage. Many tenants, even with a professional inventory, will take digital photographs or video footage of all areas of the property; these can then be used later in case of any disputes as they have the facility to record the time and date they were taken.

It is not difficult to compile your own inventory; look at each area or room of the house, including the garden and any outbuildings and make a note of condition. To ensure you have everything covered, start from the front garden and work inwards. In each room look at the door, then ceiling, walls, skirting boards and floor. Then check the furniture. Take a look at the following examples and see how easy it is to apply the appropriate descriptions to your own property.

Case History

My company was booked to carry out the checking-out procedure for some tenants who had lived in a property for two years. The agent confirmed that there had never been an inventory made to list the condition of the contents, fixtures and fittings. However, they did produce a handwritten report, of only two pages, that the tenant had thoughtfully supplied himself, signed and dated, when he moved in.

Without further evidence of condition from any other source it was this document that my company used to assess the damage made and cleaning needed, things that are normally chargeable to the outgoing tenant. Without this helpful list, albeit an amateur one, it would have been impossible to know just how dirty the house was at the start of the tenancy. This tenant had protected his security deposit by making his own inventory that was accepted by the agent and landlord from the start.

FRONT GARDEN:	Grass needs cutting, borders weedy (or all tidy if appropriate)
FRONT DOOR:	Large dent to base, one pane of glass broken, chipped to edge
HALLWAY:	Walls badly marked on the left, four hooks, three screw holes Carpet grubby through walkway
LOUNGE:	Ceiling: water stain near door Walls: few scuffs to mid level on left, three nail holes One double socket cracked

	Lampshade dirty, light not working
KITCHEN:	Walls: tiles greasy in places
	Worktops: many knife marks, several small chips
	Floor: large tear near washing machine, burn mark near oven
	Kitchen units: all need further cleaning, one shelf water-damaged

Note your appropriate observations for each room in the property and write down descriptions of any damage and anything that needs cleaning. Remember, a little work carried out now will protect your deposit. Always be realistic, don't try to be too smart by listing things in a far worse condition than they actually are. Neither the agent nor the landlord is likely then to accept your version of the condition of the house. Whatever you produce by way of your own inventory must stand up to careful checking by other individuals. It is likely that the landlord will pay you a visit to check that your comments are correct if he is to accept the inventory and abide by the comments at the end of your tenancy.

Send a signed and dated copy of the inventory to the landlord or his agent, with copies of photographs if appropriate. This is your proof of the condition of the property at time of check-in. This document should help to ensure that you are not charged for any damage that was already done when you moved in. Always remember to keep copies yourself of anything you are posting. Keep them in a safe place until you need to move out. Should there be any disputes you will have all the proof you need to stop any arguments later.

The Finer Details
If the agent or landlord doesn't have the contact details of your service suppliers you will find the addresses and telephone numbers in your local telephone directory.

Electricity
Always make a note of the electricity meter reading on the day you move in. You will then need to telephone the electricity supplier informing them that you are the new occupier and the starting meter reading. This ensures that you won't pay for any electricity used before you moved in.

Gas
Again, make a note of the meter reading as above and inform the service company of your occupancy.

Water
If your property has a water meter, carry out the same procedure. Water meters, though, can sometimes be hard to find. I'm sure that they really are a good invention but the good people at the water companies did not seem to think that anyone other than their own staff would ever need to find and read the meters. Water company officials don't need to dig up drains or poke about too much, they usually have a magic electronic scanner that, when pointed in the general direction of a meter, will give them a reading on their LCD display screen. For the rest of us poor mortals who need to take readings, we have to ask the landlord or agent about the location of the meter. If he can't help, you may need to be a bit of a detective. Water meters can be found in any one of a number of places! Yours could be in your flat, perhaps under the sink, in a communal meter cupboard somewhere in your building, in a circular drain in the driveway or path to the front of your property or, if you are moving into a block of flats, look for a rectangular drain cover which will contain several meters. If the meter for your property is not clearly marked you will need to take note of all the meter readings you can see and the reference numbers on the meters. With this information the water company will know exactly which is your meter and therefore how much you need to be charged.

By carrying out these checks you will ensure that you only pay for services from the start of your own tenancy – not for charges left over from the previous occupier. Of course, the same applies with your council tax and telephone line.

Having utility bills with your name and address on them will prove to be useful in other ways – provided that you pay them on time and don't fall into arrears. They can be used as proof of identity when you want to provide evidence of where you live – if you want to join a gym, apply for some other membership or even for a mobile phone, or if you should wish to apply for a loan or mortgage at some time in the future.

You can be sure that many times during your life your credit rating will need to be checked – if you are renting through a letting agent this will already have been done – there are things that you can do during your tenancy to make sure that your credit score stays in good shape.

- Make sure you are on the electoral roll; failure to do this can cause the biggest damage to your credit score. Ask for a form from your local district council offices

- Don't move house too often; if you live in the same place for three years your credit rating will be much better

- Don't apply for several credit cards in a short space of time. Your credit rating file, held by several national recognised agencies, will show each enquiry and the conclusion will be that you are unreliable with or short of money.

Organising Your Finances

If you are sharing, it's a good idea either to set up a separate 'house account' or at the very least ensure that everyone pays his or her share of the rent by standing order to the agent or landlord. This will guarantee that the rent is paid on time and cut down on any arguments amongst your fellow tenants.

Case History

I rented a property to a group of young account-
ants, both male and female, in their early twenties.
They set up a separate bank account for their
household expenses. Every month, by standing
order, they each paid in their portion of the rent,
and a set amount for service bills (gas, electricity
and water). They stayed in the property for two
years and everything went along very smoothly –
until two of the group decided to move elsewhere
with their respective partners at which time I lost
some of the best tenants I have ever had.

Unwanted Items Left in the House

Once you move in you may find various things tucked
away in cupboards that belong to the landlord but for
which you have no use. If you have your own kitchen
equipment or bed linen, for example, you may not want
to use any of the landlord's items that have been
supplied in the house. One option is to call the letting
agent or landlord and ask if unwanted items can be
removed. Occasionally this is possible but more usually
the landlord will not have anywhere to store them either!

If there is a cupboard somewhere in the property where
you can store these safely until you move out then just
pack the offending items away in boxes or plastic bags.
Remember though that all items must be returned in good
order to their correct locations at the end of the tenancy.
If anything does become damaged during storage (i.e. bed
linen which has suffered mould damage due to being
stored in a damp garage or shed) it is the tenant's
responsibility to supply suitable replacements otherwise
compensation costs will be deducted from the security
deposit at the end of the tenancy for payment to the
landlord.

Apart from the normal contents of a house it is quite common for landlords to leave all sorts of rubbish – too many pots of paint, clothes or boxes of personal effects, for example, that they don't have room for in their new home. They expect their tenants to store these items free of charge! According to the terms of your tenancy agreement you are not lawfully allowed to remove any items from the property without written permission.

Case History

Some tenants had received permission from the landlord to pack kitchen equipment in boxes and store them in the cellar. During the tenancy the landlord decided to visit the property, without telling the tenants, to collect something she had left behind. During her search in the cellar she dropped one of the storage boxes breaking several pieces of her own stored dinner service. Although the blame was pointed at the poor tenants, the landlord was, in fact, responsible for the damage. The tenants had her permission in writing for the storage and, as she had visited the property without their knowledge, they were unable to tell her which boxes were fragile.

The easiest way to deal with this problem is firstly to advise the landlord or his agent in writing that you would like these items removed as soon as possible. You can request that the landlord finds some other place of storage as they are restricting your use of the property. You should then state that you will not be held responsible for the safety of any such items not specifically listed on the inventory. In this way the landlord knows exactly where he stands and you are covered. Remember though that unless any item is unsafe or poses some kind of health hazard, your landlord is under no obligation to remove it from his property. Spare pots of paint may come in handy later if you need to make good any marks you have made on the walls or woodwork.

6

HAVE A PROBLEM-FREE TENANCY

The most common causes of eviction are: damage to the property, violence, abusive or unacceptable behaviour, excessive noise and, of course, non-payment of rent! While these things sound excessive it never ceases to surprise me just how many tenants fall foul of one or more of these reasons for eviction.

Looking at many tenants and the problems that they come across during their tenancies, it's easy to believe that renting is a tricky business. It isn't. As a human being you have a choice about how you behave and how you run your life. If you look around you at the way other people live you will notice those that live fairly peacefully, minding their own business, not causing problems for those who live around them – and those that don't. Whether you are living in your own home or someone else's property there are basic rules of living that you should abide by. This doesn't mean that you have to live the life of a recluse! There are lots of small things that you can do to make sure that you have fun but don't annoy anyone else at the same time. This is especially true when you are renting a property, when the rules of living are more than those listed on your tenancy agreement.

Pay Your Rent on Time
This seems obvious but it always surprises me just how many tenants think that they can pay the rent when they

wish. The date that your rent is due is the first day on which your tenancy began; this date is written on your agreement. It is your first and most important obligation to make sure that the landlord gets his rent on time each and every month.

The best way to ensure that rent payments are made on time – and that you stay out of trouble – is to set up a standing order with your bank. It's tempting to offer to send a cheque each month but this can be easily forgotten and you won't usually get a receipt for the payment.

You should always avoid paying your rent in cash either to the landlord directly or to the letting agent. This can sometimes be a dangerous practice and if you really can't avoid it now and again make sure that you get a signed and dated receipt from whomever you are paying your cash to. Always keep this receipt in a safe place until after you have moved out and your security deposit has been refunded. If using cash transactions it is easy for a landlord to deny that all payments have been made and try to deduct money from your deposit at the end of the tenancy.

Standing order is by far the safest way of making any payments. You will have a legally acceptable proof of payment should there be any disputes later. Setting this up is simple; you just need to let your bank know the details of the person to whom you are paying the rent: the name and address of their bank, account number, sort code and the date and amount of the payment. If you are using the services of letting agents, they will normally have standing order forms pre-printed to enable you to fill in the blanks with the relevant information.

Settling In

Naturally you will want to make the place your own – at least for the time you intend to live there. Before you start sticking up those posters or hanging your favourite photographs or paintings just stop and think. The property belongs to someone else and any damage to the interior walls will have to be made good when you leave. Before

> **Pat's Top Tip**
> Sometimes the date that your salary is paid into your bank may not coincide with the rent due date. If you are paid at the end of the month you could suggest that you pay a little extra the first month and then start the standing order a day or so after payday. This means that if your rent is due on the 15th of the month and your salary is paid on the 30th you need to pay an extra 15 days' worth of rent initially to bring your next and subsequent monthly payment date up to the end of the month. This will ensure that you have money in the bank at the right time to pay what is due.

you start banging in picture hooks and pins you will need to get written permission – unless you are using existing holes. It seems petty but the standard charge at the end of a tenancy is usually about £5 per nail hole to make good. This figure takes into account the cost of a painter going to the property with filler and matching paint to cover up the damage. This relatively minor damage will soon add up to a lot of your deposit money.

On the same subject, beware of sticking posters to walls. Sticky tape and blue/pink/white tack may seem to be a great solution but all of these leave greasy marks on the wall and may even damage the surface when you try to remove them after a few months. (Not quite so damaging to woodwork so if your property has picture rails you may yet be able to hang those posters.)

Going to extremes (outrageous but true): A tenant living in a ground floor flat decided to expand his living space. So, without permission from the landlord, he demolished a joining wall to make the lounge and dining

Case History

Four students moved into a house and promptly covered most of the interior walls with posters. One lad was a Liverpool fan and stuck every kind of club memorabilia on his bedroom wall that he could get his hands on. When they moved out at the end of the tenancy the whole bedroom and several of the rooms in the rest of the house had to be redecorated at the tenants' expense. Although the interior decoration was not especially good at the start, by the time the tenants had stripped the walls of their posters and souvenirs they had left many small greasy marks, tears and pinholes throughout the property. The landlord was within his rights to demand that the walls were 'made good' and got a complete redecoration into the bargain at the tenants' expense.

room into one large room. Unfortunately, it was a supporting wall and the ceiling collapsed bringing the contents of the first floor flat above crashing into his lounge. The landlord – or his insurance company – had to pay out over £12,000 to make both flats habitable again. The tenant was quoted as saying that he had no intention of moving out! Hopefully this tenancy was covered by an assured shorthold agreement – I bet his landlord couldn't wait to serve notice on him.

Consider Others

Tenants often have their own unique and sometimes strange views of how the average person lives. Opinions differ as to whether it is acceptable to have loud parties every Saturday night, leave your dog barking all day while you are out at work or store heaps of revolting rubbish in your front garden while you wait to come up with a good idea about how to get rid of it.

Just pretend for a moment that you are your neighbour, you are living next door to someone like yourself. How would you cope? Getting along in life is all about giving some measure of consideration to other people; in the case of a tenant, this usually means not only whoever is sharing the house with them but the people who live in surrounding properties – their neighbours.

The more formal rules of living are those listed in your tenancy agreement. These are your minimum obligations when living in a rented property. If you keep an eye on these things then you will go a long way towards enjoying a problem-free tenancy.

Don't Be a Nuisance to Your Neighbours
Try to be considerate when parking cars. Don't park over someone's driveway or obstruct the pavement. Remember people have wheelchairs, prams and pushchairs, are blind or could have any number of other problems or disabilities and being unable to walk on the pathway could cause them injury – and damage your car.

Parties are great, but not usually for your neighbours – unless of course you invite them too. It's polite to inform your neighbours of what you are planning even if they are not invited; they might choose to go out for the night and come back when it's all over and peace has returned. Try to keep things down to a dull roar.

Normal late night noise can be irritating to your neighbours: slamming car doors, loud voices, drunken singing; all the usual culprits that result in arguments with those around you. Remember, if you are in breach of your tenancy agreement in any way, the landlord has a legal right to terminate your tenancy and evict you.

Nosy Neighbours and Your Right to Privacy
Neighbours, on the other hand, can be just as irritating!

Case History

One property I managed for several years was looked over by a concerned neighbour. I had regular telephone calls from him to report the behaviour of my four (very well behaved) tenants. So called misdemeanours included: too many cars parked in the road (there were two in the drive and one on the road!), one tenant's company van was parked outside ('spoils the view' he complained, 'no-one else in the road has a van') and the best moan from this chap, who obviously had a very empty life, was that the tenants were hanging their shirts on the bedroom curtain rail which looked untidy when he looked out of his windows. Unless there was actual damage to property or real nuisance occurred, none of these would be in breach of the tenancy agreement.

It is quite usual for neighbours to hold a key to your property. When a landlord lets his house, especially if it is for the first time he will often make sure that a friendly neighbour has a key 'for emergencies'. There is not too much that you can do about this except ask for assurance that the neighbour will not use his key without your permission.

Sadly, it is not uncommon for a neighbour (or a landlord) to feel that he can come and go as he wishes while you are living in the property. This is against the terms of your tenancy agreement. This states that you, as a paying tenant, must be allowed 'quiet enjoyment' of the property you are renting. If this happens to you, write to your landlord stating that this is unacceptable and access should only be arranged by appointment and in writing. If the situation continues you could even prosecute your landlord for harassment. However, most things can be discussed and resolved calmly. Legal action should only ever be a last resort after everything else has failed.

It should be a sobering thought that, as tenants, you will most certainly be watched over by someone close by. Most streets have their own 'neighbourhood watch' whether official or not! You can be sure that should things get out of hand some kind soul will inform your agent or landlord about your behaviour if deemed necessary. Big Brother is undoubtedly watching you.

One property that I had dealings with had a problem with a neighbour who was a long-standing friend of the landlord and his family. This neighbour had been given a key when the house was let with instructions to keep an eye on the place – even though the property was fully managed by a letting agent. At various times during the tenancy I would get a call from the tenants to say that odd items had appeared in their garage. First it was a mountain bike, then a garden table and chairs; the garage seemed to be a very handy storage facility. This went on for some time; the tenants were very relaxed about it until it suddenly dawned on them that the neighbour had to go through the house to get access to the garage! Obviously this was unacceptable, the neighbour in question was sent a polite but firm letter pointing out the error of his ways. If this problem had continued I would probably have arranged to change the locks on the access door rather than prosecute the neighbour – a more effective and much faster solution.

Tips to Safeguard Your Deposit
Redecorating
Although the house or flat you are renting will be your home for at least the next six months, always remember that, because it is owned by someone else, you do not have a given right to do whatever you wish. If you hate the colour of the walls you can't just repaint them whatever

colour you choose. If the landlord has painted his rooms purple or lime green and you can't live with the colour try the following steps:

1. First ask your landlord if he would consider repainting to tone the place down a little. (Try not to be too rude about his choice of decoration even if it is pretty outrageous.) If his answer is no, don't give up.

2. Next, try asking if you can do the job yourself and perhaps he could pay for the paint. If all else fails go to step 3.

3. Ask if you can repaint if you buy the materials for yourself.

On the other hand, if your choice of colour is a little unusual don't be surprised if you are asked to return the room(s) to the original colour at the end of the tenancy. If you don't do this you will be charged for a professional painter to do the work after you have left – as with all things this will be rather more expensive than if you had done it yourself.

There are other ways in which you can try to safeguard your deposit. Mostly these are just common sense but a little reminder now may save you money later.

In the Kitchen

● Don't cut bread directly on kitchen work surfaces. Knife marks are a common problem when assessing charges for damage and will cost you dearly. Anything from £10 to £150, depending on the extent of the damage, could be deducted from your deposit later if you have marked a section of worktop. Always use a chopping board. Hot saucepans can burn worktops and damage the surface – use a heatproof pan stand.

Case History

A couple of tenants moved into a cottage which had a bedroom painted in deep purple. They asked for permission to paint the wall magnolia, at their own expense. The landlord confirmed that this could be done to a satisfactory standard. When the time came for them to move out it was found that the repainted walls were too thinly painted and although the room looked much cleaner and brighter than before, the landlord was allowed to charge the tenants for repainting the room properly in his choice of colour. This seems unfair on the poor tenants but this is just what can happen if a landlord wishes to stick to the letter of the law. A tenant's 'satisfactory standard' may not be the same as the landlord's.

- If you have a ceramic hob, make sure that you only use specialist cleaning liquids since scouring powders will damage the surface. Only flat-bottomed pans should be used on these hobs. If these are not supplied by the landlord and the hob is listed as damaged on the check-out report then you should not be held liable. The landlord should have supplied the correct equipment.

- Electric cookers and hobs with solid rings: try to wipe these over daily; they are prone to rust easily in a short space of time. I continually meet tenants who have been charged for the cost of a new hob for the sake of a little ongoing cleaning.

- In areas of hard water there can be a build-up of limescale everywhere. It's prudent to use cleaning products containing a descaler (easily available from your local supermarket) in your kitchen and bathroom – if a cleaning company is sent in at the end of the tenancy the costs will be considerable.

Pat's Tip: cut a lemon in half and rub on any areas of limescale, this will melt away the scale and bring back some shine.

- Beware of acrylic sinks. Why these are ever put into rented properties I will never know. They scratch, melt and stain very easily. Hot saucepans should not be rested anywhere on the surface, they will cause melt marks for which you will be charged later. Knives thrown into the washing up bowl – a common practice – can cause cut marks to the sink, another cost to you later.

- Vinyl flooring is easily damaged. Take care if you need to move any kitchen appliances as dragging out a washing machine or fridge can tear the surface, stiletto heels also cause small holes to this kind of flooring.

In the Bathroom

- Make sure that the bathroom is well ventilated. This doesn't mean that you have to freeze while you are having your bath, just try to avoid a build-up of condensation. If there is an extractor fan make sure you switch it on. If it's noisy, tenants are tempted to keep it turned off but in the long run, you could be encouraging heavy condensation which will cause blackening on the ceiling, walls and window frames. If this is allowed to continue throughout your tenancy you will be liable for the cost of redecorating the whole room. Try to leave the door open when you are not in the room or leave the window vents open. Wipe over the windows and frames if they look wet. If you are using the shower make sure you use the shower curtain properly. Tuck the hem into the bath; if you leave it to hang outside the bath the water will just run onto the floor, causing staining and damage. Just a few small precautions that will save you a lot of money at the end of the tenancy.

A common problem which lots of tenants fall foul of is that they assume all showers can be used as showers! If the bathroom walls are not fully tiled, especially around the bath area, and the bath has a shower fitting on a mixer tap this usually means that it is for hand-held use only. If there is no shower bracket high up on the wall don't try to use the shower standing up in the normal position. Water will cause damage to the painted section of the wall above the tiling and you will be liable for redecoration later.

Other Problem Areas

- Try to use a mattress protector. A recent cost to an out-going tenant was for replacing a double mattress. After a heavy rugby match, the tenant's sporting wounds bled during the night and the new mattress was ruined. An accident, of course, but ultimately the tenant must take responsibility for this kind of damage and will have to pay compensation to the landlord.

- Hot coffee cups or spilt drinks are another costly problem when they have been left on a polished table or shelf. Any resulting ring marks will have to be polished out at the end of the tenancy. The minimum charge for a French polisher is around £70 – no matter how small the job.

- Leather suites need particular leather cleaning creams and certain woods used in the manufacture of tables and other furniture items require special polish. Often the landlord will leave you the appropriate cleaning materials if he has supplied specialist furniture. If this kind of furniture is part of your let and needs to be specially looked after then you should be provided with the cleaning products to enable you to do so.

- Never iron clothes directly on the carpet. Most modern carpets contain a high percentage of man-made fibres and hot irons melt carpet pile instantly – new carpets will be expensive.

- Wooden floors are more easily marked than you might think. Again, stiletto heels can cause large areas of damage. In another recent dispute, the tenant was charged for replacement of a whole lounge floor after it was discovered that heel marks had caused large areas of small indentations to the wood. Although the damage was accidental the tenant was still liable.

- A little word of warning about house plants left by the landlord. You are not legally responsible to keep plants alive. After all, if they are particularly rare or expensive they should not have been left in the house to take their chances with tenants who may or may not be interested in plants. If they die you should just leave the plant pots in place when you leave. If you are a plant lover make sure that you wipe up any spills as water damages woodwork and furnishings. Be especially careful when watering large, floor-standing plants. Make sure that the water is not seeping onto the carpet under the pot as this is a major cause of damage and, therefore, deductions from your deposit. When you move the pot some time later you could find a large stain under the bottom, or worse, the carpet could be rotted under the pot and you will be liable for the cost of a replacement carpet.

Case History

Recently some tenants were checked-out of their house. During the tenancy they had tried really hard to keep the owner's large plants going. They had diligently watered and fed them and washed the leaves when necessary thinking that they were doing a good job. On the check-out inspection, the inventory clerk moved the plant pot and discovered a large rotted area in the carpet. As the landlord's insurance policy did not cover accidental damage and they had no insurance at all, they ended up £500 out of pocket.

Repairs and Problems

You should have already found out just who is responsible for what regarding repairs and maintenance. Sometimes the tenancy agreement will list some extra items that the tenant is responsible for. If the landlord has supplied a washing machine or microwave oven that is fairly old, he may have put a clause in the agreement to say that he won't be responsible for the repair of these items if they should break down during the tenancy. If an item covered by this kind of clause breaks down you just have to make a decision, either pay for the repair yourself or store the broken item until the end of the tenancy.

For example, if it is a large item like a washing machine, you will either have to start using the local launderette or may need to buy your own replacement; which you will, of course, take with you when you move out at the end of the tenancy. In this case you should request that the old item is removed as soon as possible. If they do nothing, as is sometimes the case, then you will have to remove it yourself and store it in a shed or garage – or the back garden if you are desperate! (If you have to leave it outside make sure you cover it with a protective sheet of plastic; this way you won't take the chance of being penalised later by way of your deposit.) Always confirm what you are doing in writing to the agent.

Report any problems immediately to the agent or landlord.

It is in the best interests of both the tenant and the landlord that any repairs or accidents are reported as soon as they happen. This ensures that the property stays in good shape. The landlord should be more than happy to protect his investment and keep his tenants contented – provided that they are good tenants in the first place.

There may even be a clause in your agreement that states 'the tenant should immediately report any damage or disrepair, defect or deficiency in the property or to the contents, and may be held liable for any costs arising from failure to report such defects and to pay repairs or make good necessary if further damage should occur through misuse or neglect by the tenant'.

In practice this means that come the end of your tenancy if, for example, you had never reported that the guttering had been leaking badly and over a period of time there was serious water damage to the patio, you could be liable for the cost of repairs – not only to the guttering, but for relaying the patio when you have vacated. Always think of things in terms of cause and effect. See Case History overleaf.

It is not usually recommended that tenants carry out repairs themselves. If they are not good at DIY then there is a danger that a professional maintenance person will have to make good at a later date – at the tenant's cost. But there are lots of small things that tenants can do for themselves. Just because you are renting someone else's property don't think that you are not responsible for changing your own light bulbs or for small but useful things like re-sticking seams of wallpaper that start to peel or tightening screws of cupboard doors before they fall off completely. I have had several tenants over the years

---

Case History

During one tenancy the bath seal was faulty and in need of replacement. The tenants didn't report this and water from the shower leaked down the side of the bath and badly stained the kitchen ceiling below. Over the course of a couple of months the ceiling became mouldy and started to bubble. The tenants ignored this completely so that when they finally moved out they were charged for the full cost of replacing the ceiling and making good the damage – a very expensive process which could have been easily avoided if they had just made that telephone call to request that the bath seal be renewed a few weeks earlier – or even attempted to repair it themselves. Their negligence was deemed to have caused greater damage to the property than would normally have occurred had they acted faster.

---

calling to request help when light bulbs blow or the trip switch of the fuse box pops out!

There are lots of small maintenance jobs that need to be done when you are living in a property that are all the responsibility of the tenants. Things like: changing fuses, light bulbs, draught excluder around door frames, sorting out dripping taps (usually just a washer to change but you may need to pay for a plumber!), keeping drains clear and free-running and repairing broken windows (if you have caused the damage). It's no good ringing your letting agent for help with any of the above; he will give you a very short answer!

Contractors' call-out charges are very expensive and if you have not carried out any of the more obvious checks before making that call, you will be liable for any costs incurred.

Case History

I received a call from some tenants late one night to report that the central heating was not hot enough and could I arrange for an engineer to call. They had lived in the property for more than a year so I asked them if they had tried to bleed the radiators to make sure there was no air in the system. They said they had. We then talked about temperatures and thermostats, "We haven't got a thermostat", I was told. Patiently I explained that if they went into the hallway and looked on the wall they would find a small square box with a dial and numbers marked on it. Off they went, amazed to find the thermostat sitting there all along set on 15 degrees. They turned it up to 25 degrees – heating problem solved!

Here are a few of the more common problems encountered by tenants and suggestions for the immediate action you can take. If this does not work then you will need to call for help.

- NO COLD WATER SUPPLY: usually due to some kind of maintenance work locally. Check with your neighbours to see if they are in the same position, or check with the local water supply company. They will have information about any local problems

- NO ELECTRICITY: if the whole house is cut off (and you have paid your bills) check with the neighbours to see if others are affected, if not, check your fuse box. It may be that you have overloaded the system somehow by perhaps plugging in too many appliances on the same circuit

- COLD RADIATOR: check for trapped air or low pressure in the system by using a small radiator key to 'bleed' the radiator

- BLOCKED DRAINS: caustic soda is good for clearing sink wastes (available in any hardware store) or any of the proprietary brands on sale. The best treatment is to try and avoid the problem and flush only liquids down your sinks

- INOPERATIVE APPLIANCES: check the fuses in the plug or fuse box and check the power supply and controls to the appliance. Read the instruction manual if there is one. It is surprising how many tenants do not bother to read the basic instructions before calling for help

- LEAKING OR DEFROSTING FRIDGE: check the power supply and controls. Check also the internal drain hole. This is usually found inside the back and towards the bottom of the fridge

- GAS: do not take any chances. If you smell gas and suspect a leak do not turn on any electrical switches or ignite naked flames. Open all doors and windows and turn off the gas stopcock, which is usually located beside the meter. You should then immediately call the local gas emergency telephone number, listed in your telephone book under 'GAS'.

  The property will have a copy of the gas safety certificate for your records; this doesn't guarantee that all the appliances will work perfectly for the next twelve months. If you have any suspicions that an appliance is dangerous call the gas company immediately. Things to keep a watch for are:

- Any sooty marks noticeable on or around any appliances

- Gas flames that suddenly burn yellow or orange in colour, instead of blue

- Solid fuels that seem to burn slowly or go out suddenly.

If you or your housemates are feeling a little unwell you should be aware of the signs and symptoms of carbon monoxide poisoning. These are:

- Sickness and diarrhoea

- Unusual chest pains or stomach pains

- Headaches

- Unexplained drowsiness or feeling giddy when standing up

If you experience any of these problems call the gas company, open windows and doors to ventilate the property and avoid a build up of leaking gas. Don't stay inside the house for any longer than you have to.

Your Landlord's Responsibilities
If the central heating boiler or the washing machine should break down under an assured shorthold lease it is the landlord's responsibility to organise repairs; unless, of course, the damage was caused by tenant abuse. If you cause something to break down or to be damaged, it is your own responsibility to pay for the repair.

If your landlord is reluctant to attend to any general repair problems during your tenancy, don't panic. If you can't seem to get any action you should inform the landlord or his agent in writing of the nature of the problem and request urgent attention. Do not stop paying your rent. This is unlawful and you will be in breach of your tenancy agreement.

The next step would be to get yourself two estimates for the work that is needed, send these to the landlord or agent with a covering letter explaining that if you do not hear from him and no action is taken in a specified time (for example, this could be seven days) you will organise the contractor to make the necessary repair, pay the bill and deduct the amount from your next month's rent. This will usually spur landlords into action or at the very least you can then organise the repair. The cost of repairs should not exceed the amount of one month's rent.

Allowable waiting times for repairs are usually:

24 hours for no hot or cold water, heat or electricity or any problem hazardous to life.

72 hours for appliance repairs: oven, fridge or major plumbing fixture.

10 days for any other repairs.

Of course, you do have other options if you are faced with landlords or agents who will not uphold their responsibilities regarding repairs.

● ARBITRATION OR LITIGATION: you could consult a solicitor and go to court to try and force the landlord into action. Or the dispute can be settled by an arbitration service if the landlord will agree. This is usually cheaper (and faster) than going to court

● MOVE OUT: this is a last resort. If you have given the landlord written notice of the repairs needed and waited the necessary time with no result, you can lawfully give written notice and move out. Make sure that your rent is paid up to date and the utility bills are settled. In this situation tenants are entitled to receive a refund of any rent overpaid and any security deposit due. However, this is a risky move as once you have left the property it could be a long and painful process to get back any money that the landlord is holding.

Your Responsibilities

Keep the house clean and tidy. No one expects tenants, or anyone else, to live in a show house. However, it is not unreasonable to expect a fair standard of cleanliness. The letting agent will arrange to inspect your property at three-monthly intervals. If your living standards are exceptionally bad you can expect a strong warning letter in the next post.

There are good reasons why certain standards are unacceptable in a rented property. Just think about it; if discarded food is left lying around for days on end (or even overnight in warm weather) this will encourage vermin. I remember reading somewhere recently that at any time of the day or night we are all no further than one metre away from a rat! On a more mercenary level you could also be financially liable for any damage caused by pests during your tenancy.

Anything from flies and other insects to mice and rats will enjoy dining in your home if you leave enough rubbish about the place. These can not only bring disease, which affects humans, but mice and rats are quite happy to chew through electrical wiring, make their nests in furniture and generally cause havoc and great expense.

When tenants leave a property early they must still be able to take care of the condition of the house and its contents and also leave the place clean and free of rubbish. It is sensible in these cases to talk to the agent or landlord or perhaps to give a key to a friendly neighbour who can pop in regularly and check that everything is OK. An empty house is inviting, so guard against squatters – either human or animal.

Pest Control – Your Responsibilities

While we are on the subject of pests, there are some things that are outside of your control but which you will need to

---

Case History

Some tenants left their house three weeks before the end of their tenancy without informing their letting agent, leaving the place dirty with all kinds of rubbish left behind. This was a relatively new house with new furniture on a new development. During the time the house was empty a family of dormice moved into the lounge. They ate their way through the base of the settee and set up a comfortable home there. When the tenants returned on the day of the check-out both the lounge and two of the bedrooms were affected by the mice infestation. Several items of (new) furniture were damaged and a couple of carpets too. As the tenants were still legally responsible for the property until the day of their check-out, which was the last day of the tenancy according to their agreement, they had to pay for all the cleaning and for making good all the damage.

---

act upon. Some things are part of your responsibilities as a tenant and some are the landlord's. Who pays for what is a confusing issue but here are a few clues:

Wasps
Should you be unlucky enough to have a wasps' nest somewhere in the property, it will be your responsibility to arrange/pay for its removal. The first course of action is to telephone your local council; their pest control officer can arrange for treatment and removal of the nest. Or, of course, you could check out your local *Yellow Pages* directory for one of the many private companies who carry out this service. The cost will be around £40. If, of course, the wasps' nest was already there when you moved

in, it is the landlord's responsibility to pay for its removal. You should report the problem on moving-in day; any later and it could be argued that the wasps have only just arrived and are therefore your responsibility.

Bees
Bees are a protected species and swarms should only be removed by a professional bee-keeper. It is the responsibility of the tenant to pay for removal. Again, the council or your local directory will provide you with some names and telephone numbers.

Bats
Any nesting of bats in your belfry – or even your roof – will have to be ignored! Bats are also a protected species but must be left to their own devices. Generally, they will not cause too much damage but their droppings can be fairly disgusting. Good for plants and, in some countries, even used for fuel but probably not recommended. If you have these visitors in your house report it to your landlord immediately – and buy some ear plugs!

Squirrels
These are a real nuisance and can cause serious damage if they should decide to explore your loft. Squirrels are known to chew through just about anything; electrical wiring is a particular delicacy. If they get into your house they will run around and make a real mess. If you see squirrels running about your garden take a few sensible precautions. Keep your bedroom windows closed, especially if you are not at home. Squirrels are very nosy creatures and can't resist exploring. Another sensible precaution is to keep trees and bushes trimmed back well away from the house as squirrels are very agile and can jump quite long distances to get on to your roof or walls. If you hear early morning scrabbling noises in your roof and there are squirrels about in your vicinity then you are in trouble. Call your landlord or agent immediately; it is

illegal to trap and kill squirrels during their breeding season but, unfortunately, this is just the time when they want to inhabit your home. You will need to consult a pest control company who can advise you of the best way to proceed. They can set traps in the roof, repair any access holes and inspect the loft for signs of activity over a set period of time.

Ants

These can be a real nuisance and will return, usually to your kitchen, time and again to plague you. It is your responsibility to treat this problem and it is fairly simple. There are a hundred and one (and probably more) treatments available from supermarkets or hardware shops. The most sensible treatment is to make sure that all surfaces/floors are kept clean and free from crumbs or food particles. Be careful when using ant powder or liquids, especially if you have pets or young children, as these treatments are poisonous and should be placed out of reach of pets and children.

Mice

Again, sensible food hygiene rules apply to discourage them. Danger times are usually in the autumn when their outside environment is becoming colder and they seek warmer nesting places before winter sets in. If you can't keep a cat to help you out there are several ways to keep them in check available from hardware stores and supermarkets. Mousetraps and poison are the usual deterrents or there are, of course, more humane traps available to enable you to catch the mouse and release it several miles away!

Rats

If this is an ongoing problem with the property, it is the landlord's responsibility to pay for regular treatment. It is possible to take out a contract with a local pest control company who will set traps at various sites around the

---

Pat's Top Tip

A small tip from an experienced mouse catcher: their favourite treat, and very useful for using in traps, is chocolate rather than cheese. You will get good results by setting your traps with chocolate digestives (preferably those famous Scottish sounding ones!).

---

house and garden and make a monthly call to check and re-bait and also to monitor activity. However, if rats suddenly appear during the tenancy it's up to you to organise pest control. The same rules apply as for mice infestations (see previous section).

Fleas

If you suffer from a flea infestation, immediately upon moving in report the problem to your agent or landlord; it is his responsibility to have the carpets and upholstery fumigated if your animals are not the cause of the problem. Again, there are professionals who provide treatment for this problem. If action is not taken fast enough, and it's you who has to live with it, don't panic. You will just need to buy a couple of aerosol sprays of flea treatment from your local supermarket and thoroughly spray all areas of the house. Full instructions are on the can but usually this has to be left for a couple of hours before vacuuming throughout. Treatment can be repeated periodically as necessary. OK, enough scratching now!

Garden Maintenance

Even if you are not the slightest bit interested in the outdoor life, if your property has anything resembling a garden and it was in a reasonably tidy condition when you moved in, it is your responsibility to keep it tidy. This means cutting the grass at regular intervals and keeping the borders weed-free. You don't have to be a landscape gardener to keep things fairly tidy. This will save you a lot of money when you move out. It is not unknown for neighbours to contact the landlord or agent to report untidy gardens; no one likes to live next door to a scruffy house or garden!

When you move out, if the landlord has to arrange for a professional gardener to bring the place back up to speed, it can be extremely expensive. Gardeners charge anything from £15 to £20 per hour. This adds up over the course of a couple of days' work; do not under estimate how long it takes to weed borders properly!

Case History

I checked out some tenants who had lived in a house for nine months, part of which was during the spring and summer period when gardens tend to grow with gusto. They didn't cut the lawn once during the tenancy but the week before they were due to move out all the grass was hacked down. Unfortunately the weather turned very hot and the lawn quickly turned brown and died. Leaving grass long for months and then chopping it back does not produce a good lawn. These tenants were charged for re-turfing the whole lot. Not much change left from £850; not much of their deposit left either.

Going on Holiday

If the property is going to be empty for any length of time, it is your responsibility to ensure that everything is safe while you are away. It is usually a condition of the household insurance that for short periods during cold spells – any time between the beginning of November and the beginning of March is a good guideline – the heating should be left on, at a low temperature, to prevent pipes freezing and any subsequent flooding of the property.

If you are going to be away from the property for several weeks you will need to have the heating system drained down by a professional plumber. Your agent will recommend a contractor or you will need the services of a proper Corgi registered plumber. You should also leave the loft hatch open a little to allow the air to circulate. If possible, try to arrange for someone to visit the property regularly to ensure that all is well.

Be Safe
You have a responsibility as a tenant to close and lock, where possible, all windows and doors and generally ensure that the property is as secure as you can make it. You should also inform your landlord or agent that you are going on holiday. They may be able to keep an eye on the place.

If there are any problems while the house is empty which can be blamed on your neglect as a tenant to carry out any of these sensible precautions then you will be financially liable to make any repairs necessary. In the case of a burglary, it is you who will be liable for replacement of anything stolen if you have accidentally left a window open or a door unlocked while you were away.

Access for Contractors During Your Tenancy
At some time during your time in your new home you will need to allow access to other people, whether you are there or not. You should always be consulted at least 24 hours before any proposed visit, unless it is an emergency.

Gardener
For larger properties the services of a gardener could be included in the cost of the rent. He may already have a key to access the house or side gate or even be allotted a lockable shed for tools which only he has the key for. You

should be informed in advance when the gardener is due to visit and if you will need to leave a gate unlocked for access.

Cleaner
Again, it is usually only the larger properties which will have the cost of a cleaning or housekeeping person included in the rent. Someone who works entirely inside the property will have his own key to allow him to come and go as necessary. You should know in advance when he is due to visit. It's strange but true that anyone I ever knew who was lucky enough to have this kind of regular help felt the need to tidy up before the cleaner arrived.

Pat's Top Tip

If you notice any damage that has been accidentally caused by a visiting contractor always report it, by telephone and in writing, to the agent. This will cover you against any charges made from your deposit later. For example, a double-glazing company fitted new windows in a rented property but in the process accidentally broke a ceramic towel rail. The tenant didn't bother to report this – it wasn't his house after all – however, when he was checked out of the property, he was charged for the replacement and fitting of a new towel rail as there was no proof of whether it was the glaziers or the tenant who had caused the damage.

Inspections

Every three months or so, your agent or landlord will want to carry out a general inspection of the property. This visit should only take a few minutes and is needed to make sure that there are no ongoing maintenance problems – or that the tenants are not mistreating the property and therefore in breach of the tenancy agreement. Things that are checked during these visits are:

Outside the Property

- The condition of the garden – are the tenants maintaining this well?

- General appearance of the exterior of the house. If the paintwork needs attention or the guttering is damaged then the landlord will need to know so that he can rectify matters and therefore protect and maintain the standard of the property.

Inside the Property

- General standard of living of the tenants; a certain amount of untidiness and lack of housework is expected, after all they are paying rent and are entitled to relax. However, if this borders on neglect that is causing damage to the fabric of the building, this is another matter entirely.

- Ceilings are checked for any sign of damage from water staining. It's important to report any leaks immediately before things get worse.

- Bath seals and tile grouting/filler will be looked at. This needs to be in good condition to ensure that water cannot seep behind the tiles and cause damage to walls, floors and ceilings below.

- Signs of heavy condensation will be looked for. If the tenants are constantly drying washing on the radiators there could be staining on the walls or the window frames could be blackened from water damage. These kinds of things can cause serious and costly damage to the house and will need to be rectified quickly.

If there are problems noted during one of your regular inspections you will be sure to receive a polite but firm letter from the letting agent or landlord requesting that these things are put right within a set period of time and another inspection date will be arranged to ensure that you are complying with this request. If any problems continue and the tenant does nothing to improve matters, he could be in breach of the tenancy agreement and the landlord would then have grounds to start eviction proceedings.

It's in the Post
During your tenancy of a property you will undoubtedly receive many items of post that are not addressed to you. Any letters that are sent in the landlord's name should be redirected immediately, either to the letting agent or to your landlord if you have been given his address. Any letters received for any other name should be 'returned to sender'. Simply cross out the name and address and write on them 'not known at this address', put them back in the post box and forget them. This should help to ensure that the company that sent them does not make the same mistake again. If you just put everything that is not addressed to you in a drawer somewhere – as many tenants do – you could be in breach of the agreement. Most tenancy agreements will have some kind of clause that states that any mail received for anyone other than the current tenant should be redirected to the agent or landlord.

7

EXTENDING YOUR TENANCY

When you are near the end of your tenancy term, no more than sixty or less than thirty days before the end, you will be asked, in writing, whether you want to stay in the property or to move out when the tenancy agreement expires.

Notice to Quit
If the landlord is returning to the house or selling it, you will just receive a letter informing you of this and your *notice to quit – Section 21 (4) (a)* (see overleaf). Whether leaving at the end of the tenancy is your decision or because the landlord wants possession of the property, the only thing you will need to do right now is simply to arrange a convenient time on moving-out day when you can go through the check-out and return all keys. You should confirm this appointment date and time in writing to the agent or landlord. (If you are leaving then look in the following chapter where you will find everything you need to know to get ready for the check-out.)

First Time Tenant

HOUSING ACT 1988

SECTION 21 (4) (a)

ASSURED SHORTHOLD TENANCY:

NOTICE REQUIRING POSSESSION:

PERIODIC TENANCY

TO: (Name of Tenant – see note 3)

OF: (Address of Tenant – see note 3)

FROM: (Name of Landlord)

OF: (Address of Landlord)

I/We give you notice that I/We require possession of the dwelling house known as:

10 The Street,   (Address of Property)
Barfield, Sussex

AFTER: (Date of Expiry – see note 3)

DATED: (Date of Notice – see note 3)

SIGNED: (by the Landlord or his Agent)

LANDLORD/AGENT: (Name and Address of Agent if not
                               Signed by Landlord)

SIGNED: (by the Landlord)

NOTES

1. Where an Assured Shorthold Tenancy has become a Periodic Tenancy, a Court must make an order for possession if the Landlord has given proper notice in this form.

2. Where there are joint Landlords at least one of them must give this notice.

3. This notice must expire: (1) on the last day of a period of the tenancy, (2) at least two months after this notice is given, (3) no sooner than the earliest day on which the tenancy could ordinarily be brought to an end by a notice to quit given by the Landlord on the same day.

If you are happy to stay in the property and the landlord has no other plans and is happy to extend the tenancy, this can be done in either of the following ways:

Extension of Tenancy Agreement
You will receive a formal offer of the extension stating the length of the new term (as you will have discussed previously with your agent or landlord). An extension will usually be for six or twelve months, again depending on your preference.

Pat's Tip: as stated earlier, make sure that you have a break clause in your extension agreement. Usually the terms of your original tenancy agreement will still be in force and you will be issued with a one-sheet notice of extension – as shown overleaf.

You and your fellow tenants will need to read everything once again before you sign, making sure that there are no additional clauses or any extra wording that has not already been agreed with you all. If you are happy that everything is in order then sign, date and return the extension paperwork. There will usually be an additional fee payable to your letting agent for this service so you will probably need to enclose a cheque as well. Normal fees are around £35 plus VAT for an extension – quite expensive for one sheet of paper!

Statutory Periodic Tenancy
If you have confirmed in writing to your landlord or agent that you wish to continue living in the property and he has agreed but not issued you with any further extension paperwork, your tenancy will then just run on and become what is known as a Statutory Periodic Tenancy, with the same conditions as your original agreement. The period of notice for both tenant and landlord will usually be thirty days. This is still a perfectly legal tenancy and all the rules of your existing tenancy agreement are still valid and enforceable.

EXTENSION TO ASSURED SHORTHOLD TENANCY

This Memorandum of Extension is made this .... day of
.... 20..... and is supplemental to a tenancy agreement
(hereinafter called 'the Agreement') made between:
Name of Landlord ....
Address of Landlord ....
Of the one part and (name of tenant) .... of the other part
whereby it is agreed by and between the Landlord and the Tenant
that the tenancy created by the Agreement of premises at (address
of the property) ....
Should continue from Noon on the .... day of
.... 20..... to Noon on the .... day of .... 20..... at
a rental of .... per calendar month and otherwise on the same
terms and conditions as the Agreement so far as they are app-
licable to an extended tenancy and subject to additional (if
appropriate) special clause(s) as detailed hereunder.
The power to give notice to terminate the tenancy specified in
clauses 1.4 (a) and 1.4 (b) of the original tenancy agreement shall
apply from the commencement of this renewed tenancy.
Signed by the Landlord or his authorised Agent ....
In the presence of ....
Name (witness to print name as above) ....
Address ....
Signed by the Tenant ....
In the presence of ....
Name (tenant to print name) ....
Address ....

Note: By Section 24 Housing Act 1988 any extension of an Assured
Shorthold Tenancy of the same premises between the same parties
need not be for any minimum length nor is any fresh pre-grant
Notice required.

Rent Reviews
It is usually at the time of your extension that your
landlord will think about increasing the rent. If you are

using letting agents, they will advise the landlord of the appropriate increase. If the letting market is fairly static they will usually suggest that keeping the rent at the same level is a more sensible option.

If your landlord suggests a rent increase you can do a little research first. Ring a couple of local letting agents and check the local property papers to make a comparison of prices for similar properties in the same area as your own. You can then make sure that the proposed rent rise is fair. If the landlord is proposing an outrageous increase you can calmly prove that what is being suggested is well above the market average.

If all else fails you have two choices. You can move out or take immediate legal advice. Under the 1977 Rent Act there is a recognised (and ridiculously complicated) formula for calculating the limit of any increase, which a solicitor or other qualified adviser can explain to you and help you put your case to the landlord. Some solicitors will give a free thirty-minute advisory session before charging you for their services; you can check this out by finding details of local solicitors in the *Yellow Pages* or, of course, by recommendation. The other and sometimes better option is to consult the Citizens Advice Bureau – their contact details are listed in the telephone directory or your local library. Their service is completely free and they have qualified advisers who can simplify the relevant details of housing law; the CAB can also help with writing letters and preparing any other documentation you may need. You need to think about whether it is better to fight or take flight. If you are happy where you are, it may be worth your time and energy trying to persuade the landlord of the error of his ways; if not, then your choice is to find somewhere else to live. If you are paying a fair market price for the rent of your property, the landlord will undoubtedly find it very difficult to get new tenants to pay a higher rent – perhaps it is worth pointing out this fact to him during your negotiations.

Subletting

At this or any other time during the tenancy you may think that it's a good idea to have someone else to share the property with you, to help with the rent and other expenses. Subletting unofficially is against the terms of your existing tenancy agreement but your agent or landlord can draw up a new agreement to include any suitable new tenants. Be aware though that this will begin a completely new term of the tenancy and you will be tied in to another minimum of six months. Credit and employment references will need to be chased for any new tenant and again there will be a fee payable to draw up a new agreement plus an additional administration fee to cover the extra work needed on chasing up references. Your new housemate will not be able to move in until he/she has been checked out thoroughly, as you yourself were at the start of your tenancy.

Sharing the Security Deposit

Any new tenants will need to contribute to the security deposit that was lodged at the start of the tenancy. If there are now two tenants instead of one, for instance, it is only sensible for the existing tenant to ask for a contribution of 50 per cent of the original security deposit. This way each tenant has an equal amount of money at stake and the responsibility for keeping the house in a good condition is also equally shared. A letter will then need to be sent by the original tenant to the agent (or whoever is already holding this money) to state that at the end of the tenancy, the deposit should be divided between both parties. If you invite another tenant to share your property and you have already paid the whole deposit to the agent, you cannot control how much damage this tenant may make for the rest of the tenancy. If he should then damage something, like a carpet or bed, for example, you will be paying for it all yourself later out of your own deposit. This is not a sensible situation to be in. Make sure that any new tenant will be financially liable in the same way that you are.

Under the terms of the tenancy agreement, tenants named on it are 'jointly and severally' responsible for a property and any payments attributable to it. If any new tenants do not have a financial stake (i.e. their proportion of the security deposit) there could be less incentive for them to take their responsibilities seriously.

Joining an Existing Tenancy
If you are not the existing tenant and are planning to join a friend's tenancy then, as mentioned earlier, the agent or landlord will need to check out your references. Your credit history and employment record will be checked; he will need to know that you can afford the rent and other outgoings. If you are not earning enough you may need to find a guarantor – someone who will promise to cover any outstanding rent should you default or run out of money.

If all goes well and you are acceptable as a tenant, it's wise to take a few precautions to safeguard your part of the security deposit. The landlord or agent will not care whether damage occurred before you moved in or not. At the end of the tenancy you will be jointly liable for any cleaning, repairs or making good that is required, regardless of the fact that someone else may have caused the problem. Joining an existing tenancy is sometimes a risky business in this respect.

It's a good idea to have a quick check through the inventory to ensure that the property is still in a similar condition as it was at the original check-in. If the current tenants have been abusing the property in any way your deposit monies will be at risk.

One of the most common problems between tenants is falling out over who is paying how much and for what, so discuss payment of bills with your other tenants before you actually move in. Decide what proportion of the gas, electricity, council tax, water, etc., you will be liable for. Try to take readings of the gas and electricity meters; it may help later if a big bill drops on the mat which covers a long period of time before you arrived at the property. Whatever you decide, get it in writing and make all the tenants sign to say they agree. The telephone is a different story. It's impossible to guess how much a phone bill will be until it drops on the mat. Make sure that the charges are itemised then you can tot up all your own calls plus your percentage of the service charges. If the bill is not set out in this way, you won't be able to tell how much you are liable for – and may end up paying for more than necessary.

When you join people who have already lived in a property for some time you may have to fit in with their routines for a while. They will be used to living together and not having to be considerate to another housemate; a little patience and compromise may be needed to make sure that all goes smoothly.

Always remember that it is better to talk than to slam doors! If you and your fellow housemates are having a few teething problems try to sit down and discuss things calmly. Everyone has different ideas about how to live so, again, sometimes a little give-and-take is needed to resolve a situation.

Whether you are extending your existing tenancy or joining others in their rented property, it is a serious commitment, both in terms of cash and responsibilities. You cannot just decide one day that you have changed your mind and leave; you can be pursued through the courts for any unpaid rent until the end of your tenancy agreement.

In reality, if an existing tenant has a falling-out with a new housemate, it can take many months of legal action to get any redress in the form of rent owed. In the meantime the existing tenant will be responsible for paying 100 per cent of the rent; the old 'jointly and severally responsible' line in the agreement comes into force leaving you legally liable for the upkeep of the property.

8

TIME TO LEAVE

Giving Notice

If you are renting through agents, they will have written to you at least sixty days before the end of your tenancy asking whether you wish to move out or stay in the property. If you intend to leave you must give notice in writing to the agent or the landlord sixty days before the end date of your tenancy, or thirty days if this falls under the terms of your statutory periodic agreement. If you fail to do this and just decide to move out earlier than you should, you will be in breach of the terms of your tenancy agreement. The landlord will be entitled to receive rent payments until the last official day of your tenancy – even if you have left the property.

Information Point

It is unlawful for you to try and use your security deposit for the last month's rent. This deposit is being held to cover any damage or cleaning needed at the end of the tenancy.

If you really need to leave earlier than the agreement allows, always discuss this with your landlord. It may be that he can find a new tenant to move in quickly, in which case you should only have to pay rent up until this new tenant's moving-in date.

Pat's Top Tip

If you are giving thirty days' notice, now is a good time to organise the mail-forwarding service with the post office. Your local post office will have details. This service usually takes three weeks to become active. You cannot expect the next tenant to forward your mail – it's more likely that, in spite of all good advice, your post will end up either sitting in a drawer for the next six months or simply in the dustbin never to be seen again. If you are really efficient, you could print out a heap of labels with your new address on, leave them in the property when you move out and you might just stand a better chance of the new tenants sending on any mail that slips through the system.

Handling Agents and Viewings

During your notice period the landlord or his agent will be advertising for new tenants. He will need to carry out viewings of the property with prospective tenants, so for the last four weeks of your tenancy, you must allow them 'reasonable' access according to the terms of your tenancy agreement. Under the terms of the Housing Act 1988, the landlord lawfully has right of ·entry to his property; provided he has given you twenty-four hours' written notice, he can enter to carry out an inspection or to make repairs.

Viewings like this should be by prior arrangement with you and at a time convenient to you. Even if you are happy for the landlord or agent to carry out the viewings in your absence you should still be consulted about appointment times. It is not acceptable for anyone to enter your rented property without any prior consultation – unless you are not contactable during the notice period for any length of time, for instance, you are away on holiday. In this case you will need to tell the agent that you are away and give your permission for access in your absence. Don't forget that even the landlord does not have the right to simply let himself into your property – except in an emergency. If he does this you should write to him making it clear that you require written notice in future of any proposed visits. If he keeps on popping in unannounced you can seek legal advice; he could be liable to prosecution for harassment and breach of your right to 'quiet enjoyment' of the property as stated in the tenancy agreement.

If the Property is For Sale
If you are moving out because the landlord is selling the property, beware of estate agents! These companies are obviously keen to make a sale and therefore earn their large commission and, in my experience, they do tend to badger tenants relentlessly for viewings at all times of the day or night. Be firm. Don't let sales agents think they have a right to arrange appointments at will and insist that they are not given a key to your property. This will only encourage them to take further liberties. If sales agents hold a key, they will not make too many attempts to call you to arrange appointments and there is a real danger that they will simply turn up at the door, letting themselves in, if necessary, in order to carry out the viewing and therefore not miss out on a potential customer! It sounds outrageous but I can confirm this is common practice throughout the industry, despite their assurances to the contrary.

Insist on twenty-four hours' notice but as in all things, try to be a little flexible. You can also refuse any appointments after 7 pm; your evenings are your own if that is what you choose.

Mostly estate agents will not accompany viewings if there is someone still living in a property. This is the easiest option for them but it is also the most risky option for you. If you are not happy to let strangers into the house then insist that the agent accompanies.

Even though you have no interest in who lives in the property once you have left, try to ensure that the place is not looking like the local tip and is in a basically clean condition during your notice period. Not only does this improve the appearance of the property but it will do no harm at this time to make a start on clearing as you go. Remember, you will need to move out in a short while and it will take longer than you realise to ensure the house is as clean and tidy as when you moved in.

Something else to think about when the landlord is selling the property: he may wish to dispose of the contents. If you are moving to another house or flat you could be interested in buying some of the items from the landlord to take with you. He, on the other hand, will probably be grateful to get rid of a few things; less for him to worry about. As usual, all things are negotiable. Try making him a fair offer for anything you think would be useful in your new home. You will probably be able to get yourself a few good bargains.

Letting agents will not usually let you know whether they have found a new tenant and re-let the property; you will only realise this when the request for viewings stops and the telephone suddenly falls silent. Once a new tenant has been found, you may be asked if you would like to vacate the property earlier than planned. If this is possible the advantage is that you will receive a refund of the remaining part of the month's rent. Alternatively, if this does not suit your plans you can, of course, simply stay until the end of the notice period.

Dealing with Threats from Your Landlord

No matter what your crime, your landlord is not lawfully entitled to throw you out with less than the legal notice period. He may want urgent vacant possession – perhaps he has had an offer from a third party to purchase the property or he has some other reason to get 'vacant possession' of his house. In any case he must serve you with the proper Notice for Possession that will state the earliest date on which he can legally ask you to move out. If no notice has been served the landlord is in breach of the conditions of the tenancy agreement. He cannot lawfully throw you out of the property just because he wishes. Should you receive any threats of this nature seek legal advice immediately; don't wait until you have been forced to leave the property. As a tenant, under an assured shorthold agreement, you have a good number of rights – including a legal right to live in the place until the end of your tenancy, as stated on the agreement.

Landlords will in some instances offer cash inducements to get a tenant to leave before the end of the tenancy. Obviously, if this is convenient to you it may be worth your while to accept the money and move on quickly. However, if leaving does not fit in with your plans, under the terms of the assured shorthold agreement you are entitled to stay put until the end of your notice period.

If you need to move out urgently for any legitimate reason you should discuss your problem with your agent or landlord. Sometimes this kind of mutual agreement can be reached between parties and, if the landlord knows that you can't cover the rent or there are other extenuating circumstances, he may wish to find a new tenant quickly and it may be possible for you to be released from your legal responsibilities.

Preparing for Moving Day

Having agreed the date and time for vacating the property you will need to take a few precautions to ensure that all your security deposit monies are returned. About two weeks before the end of your tenancy you could ask the agent or landlord to arrange to visit your property for a pre-check-out inspection. Ask if he can bring with him a checklist of his expectations, and any danger areas that you should look out for, so that you can make sure that all is in good order at the end of the tenancy. During this visit you can discuss any work needed to ensure that your deposit is returned in full.

Your first priority should be to make sure that the property is in the same condition, or better, than you found it. Get a copy of the inventory used at the time of your check-in and go through it room by room. This is a laborious process but it is vital that everything is left in the same place and condition as when you moved in. If you have moved furniture from one room to another make sure it is returned to the correct place before the day of check-out. Kitchen items can be a nightmare! A well-stocked kitchen can take you quite some time to ensure that everything is in the right cupboard exactly as the inventory decrees. Sometimes tenants will pack away much of the landlord's kitchen equipment and other items that are not needed during the tenancy. In that case, you will need to unpack them before you move out. You may think that this is a waste of time; after all, items are still in the house even if they are in different places. However, an inventory clerk will charge an additional fee to cover the time it takes him to search the property for anything he can't immediately find. This fee will be around £25 per hour. If he runs out of time or gives up without locating something, he will list it on the check-out report as missing and you will not only be charged for the cost of replacement but an additional fee to cover the cost of someone actually going to the shop to buy it.

If heavy items of furniture are in the wrong rooms on the day you check out, you could be charged for someone to visit the property after you have moved out to move these things back to their original positions. Again, a charge will be made and deducted from your deposit.

If it's possible, it's a good plan to move out a few days before the official end of the tenancy. This will give you time to make sure that the property is returned to its original condition. Cleaning, tidying and gardening are all much easier to carry out if the place is vacant with no one's personal bits and pieces getting in the way.

Cleaning Up Your Act
Please don't underestimate the importance of leaving the property in a clean condition. Any inspection carried out by the agent or the landlord when you vacate is likely to be extremely particular in respect of cleanliness. Those dusty skirting boards and cobwebs will cost dear in terms of an hourly rate from a cleaning company. A dirty cooker will cost around £60 to be cleaned professionally – cheaper to apply a little elbow grease before you leave than to be charged contractors' prices later.

Moving-out Checklist
Is the property completely clean (including every bit of the bathroom, kitchen and all paintwork)? Buy some limescale remover to make sure that all the taps and other chrome fittings are shining.

Remember: cleaning contractors are expensive. A thorough house clean will cost anything from £80 to £450 depending on the size of the property. This cost will not include cleaning carpets, upholstery or curtains.

Main Problem Areas

- Clean windows inside and out

- Wash all paintwork

- Vacuum all carpets

- Vacuum under the seat cushions of the lounge suite

Notes for Students

Remember that all tenants are 'jointly and severally' responsible for the condition of a property; everyone's deposit money is at stake. Make sure that every tenant does his or her fair share of the work. Sometimes students will clean just their own bedroom and not give too much thought to those rooms that were communal areas. Another common problem is that students may leave the property one by one over the last few weeks of the term and it is left to the last one or two tenants to clean, tidy the garden and sort out any other problems. Try to be organised; list and apportion responsibilities and make sure that everyone lends a hand. It's definitely not a good idea to throw an end of term bash just before you move out – other people's cigarette burns and wine spills will cost you dearly.

- Empty the vacuum cleaner bag!

- Launder (that means wash AND iron) all bed linen and towels if they were supplied with the property

- Make sure all surfaces are dust free – including lampshades

- Empty the filters on the washing machine, tumble drier and dishwasher

- Dry clean all curtains where necessary

- Thoroughly clean the kitchen including all appliances

- Thoroughly clean the bathroom.

Carpet Cleaning

If the carpets were in a good condition when you moved in and you have lived in a property for several months, it is a good investment to have all carpets professionally cleaned. Don't be tempted to try and save money by renting a carpet-cleaning machine and doing it yourself. This usually proves to be a false economy. It is quite common on check-out inspections to hear that the tenant has worked for hours trying to clean up the carpets only to find that most of the dirt and stains have not been removed. Nothing beats a professional steam clean. You can shop around for a good price while you are still living in the place; if you don't and it is decided that the carpets need cleaning at the end of the tenancy, it will be out of your control. An agent or landlord will not shop around and you will have to pay whatever price his own contractor decrees. It is quite usual for letting agents to add a small premium on top of the contractor's bill as 'commission' for arranging the work. This could turn out to be more expensive than a reputable cleaning company of your own choosing.

If you had permission to keep a dog or cat (or other pet) in the property, no matter how clean you think the carpets are, you will need to comply with the carpet-cleaning clause in your agreement, if there is one. All carpets and sometimes upholstery must be professionally cleaned and/or fumigated and receipts will need to be produced on the day you move out. If there is no documentary evidence available at this time, the agent or landlord will again simply organise his own contractor and the cost will be deducted from your deposit.

The same principle applies to the lounge suite. If this was in a good, clean condition when you checked in and is now looking a little the worse for wear, you should arrange for this to be professionally cleaned as well.

Garden Checklist

The garden should be left in the same condition as you found it on the day you moved in; the same condition as listed on your inventory. Obviously, if the garden looked like a building site or was very overgrown originally, the landlord cannot expect his tenants to landscape the place for the end of the tenancy. Make sure that you cannot be held responsible, and therefore charged, for anything you are not liable for:

● Mow the grass and make sure everything is tidy

● Make sure the borders are weeded and shrubs trimmed where necessary

● Don't leave heaps of garden rubbish behind; you will be charged for this to be taken away at a later date

● Sweep and tidy the garage and garden shed

● Make sure the patio and pathways are weed free.

Don't leave behind any of your own items in the property when you move out. Tenants often leave things like a chest of drawers or other unwanted furniture, empty packing boxes or old bed linen; they don't want them so they feel free just to leave them in the property. The usual course of action would be for the agent or landlord to employ someone to remove any items that do not belong to the house, at the tenant's expense.

The Inventory Check-out
Your agent or landlord will carry out this final inspection – the check-out. It will be arranged for the day you leave as at the end of the check-out, you will need to return all your keys and will not be allowed to stay in the property after that time.

Try to ensure that you are present during the check-out from start to finish. It is important that the inventory used is the same one that was checked at the start of your tenancy. It should contain all your hand-written comments and observations. Quite often a different version of the inventory is produced at check-out. This is because your original copy has been filed or lost during the tenancy; a common problem with longer lets. If you have studied the advice at the start of this book you will have your own copy safely filed away and can produce this in case of any problems.

Most letting agents employ the services of an independent inventory clerk to carry out the check-out. If the landlord is to carry out his own inspection and you are worried that this will not be an unbiased view, you can suggest that he employs a professional. (Contact details for the Association of Independent Inventory Clerks is contained in Useful Contacts.) If he is unwilling to do this, why not suggest that you pay the cost of the attendance of an inventory clerk? This will ensure that the report will be a professional, unbiased schedule of the condition of the property, noting those items which are attributable to you and those which are simply the landlord's maintenance issues. Having a professional third party is also very useful should there be any disputes at a later date.

You should always accompany whoever is carrying out the inspection during the check-out process; you need to set aside at least an hour, perhaps two, for this. There may be items that the inventory clerk cannot find which you know are in the property but are just in a different location; or there may be minor cleaning issues that you can attend to during the check-out and therefore save yourself the cost of replacements or a visit by cleaning contractors at a later date.

Wear and Tear
At the end of the check-out you should ask exactly what, if anything, you are likely to be charged for. Allowance is made for normal wear-and-tear; this translates as normal usage marks and wear to furniture, and fixtures and fittings that would be expected depending on the length of the tenancy. If you have lived in a property for two years,

the wear-and-tear allowance would obviously be more than if you had only been in a place for six months. Wear and tear does not include any cleaning issues. Opinions often differ as to what is 'normal' and acceptable wear and tear in a property, this is the best reason to make sure that a professional inventory clerk is employed. He will have the experience to judge correctly, in an unbiased manner, what you should be charged for and what is simply wear and tear or a general maintenance issue for which the landlord could be expected to cover the cost. The value of any item depreciates over time; therefore, if you accidentally damage a carpet that was new five years ago, you will be charged a percentage of the replacement cost. Wear-and-tear deductions amount to roughly 10 per cent per year. So if the carpet cost £500 five years ago, the compensation awarded to the landlord if it is damaged should be around 50 per cent, i.e. £250. Or, if you are lucky, the landlord will be able to replace the carpet under his household insurance with you, the tenant, paying only the excess on the insurance claim.

Although an inventory clerk cannot usually quote you exact costs for any damage or cleaning needed, he will be able to inform you of all items that are chargeable to you and should be able to make a very rough estimate of the cost. Now is a good time to mention any extenuating circumstances that may have a bearing on any damage for which you are likely to be charged. There could have been maintenance problems of some kind during the tenancy that have caused damage to the property, and for which you may be charged if you don't inform the inventory clerk. For example, if there are water stains on the kitchen ceiling and these are from an old leak reported during the tenancy, you must inform the inventory clerk of this fact. If you don't, there is a real danger that the staining will be reported on the check-out report. If the agent does not bother to check out the history of the tenancy, you could be charged for repainting the ceiling under the assumption that you didn't report any leak in the first place!

Another common problem that tenants can be charged for wrongly is compensation for damage that occurs when a landlord's own contractor has visited the property during the tenancy to make a repair. For example, the washing machine needs repairing and during this process, the machine has been pulled out of place and the flooring torn. If this has happened, you should have informed whoever is managing the property by telephone and in writing. You could be charged for replacing the whole of the flooring if you don't explain to the inventory clerk when you check out what happened. He will simply assume that you have damaged the floor yourself. It is not unusual for contractors to leave a small amount of damage when they have finished working; if you haven't reported it you may be penalised when you check out.

Keys

All keys for the property must be handed back to the inventory clerk, agent or landlord (or his representative) on the same day that you vacate the property. Make sure that they are listed individually and get a signed receipt. Should there be any missing or no proof that you have returned all the keys, you could be liable for the cost of either replacement keys or changing the locks; a locksmith will charge around £60 to change an ordinary front door lock, so ensuring that everything is in order will again save you a lot of money.

Closing Accounts and Final Details

Meter Readings

Take final meter readings for the gas and electricity and telephone the service companies to ask for a final bill to be sent to your new address. This will ensure that you don't pay for more supplies than you have actually used. If you forget to take meter readings or don't advise the service companies correctly or promptly, it is quite likely that you will end up paying more than you should. You will have no proof that heating or hot water left on after you have vacated the property is not actually chargeable to you.

Most meters these days have a simple numeric display. However, in older properties you will often find 'clock' meters. To read these accurately you need to start with the largest clock unit first (10,000 units) and take the number below the pointer. If the pointer is between 7 and 8 the reading for that clock is 7 and so on.

If your property has metered water you may have to hunt around a little for the meter. With any luck at all, this will be found in a small circular drain in the front pathway or driveway. If you live in a block of flats the water meter could be in a communal cupboard somewhere inside the building or, if not, look for a rectangular 'drain' cover outside which will display the water company name. A strong screwdriver will be useful as these drains are notoriously difficult to prise open. When you have finally achieved this, don't be surprised to find your meter flooded, or covered in debris or wildlife. If you really can't read the meter then call the water company and request that they take a reading urgently.

When telephoning the service companies with your closing readings, you will also need to give them your account number or the reference number that is printed on the meter. This is usually about eight numbers and a letter and will help the service companies to assign the right meter reading to your property.

Telephone
Call the telephone company to disconnect/suspend the line. By doing this you will ensure that you don't pay for someone else's telephone calls after you have left the property.

Forwarding Address
The inventory clerk or the landlord's representative will need to take details of your new forwarding address and telephone number.

Overleaf is a useful form to use at the end of a check-out, especially if the landlord is carrying out his own inspection. Fill in all the blanks with the relevant information and both you and the person who is inspecting the property should have a copy before you vacate the property. This will help to formalise things and hopefully make the landlord aware of his obligations when trying to make charges on your deposit. Provided you have at least a signed check-out report, you will have some documentary evidence of proposed deductions.

Deductions from Your Deposit
A letting agent will normally send you a copy of the formal check-out report with a detailed list of all items that you are to be charged for and the cost. If you don't receive one within a week or two of the check-out, request that one is sent to you. If you feel that the report is unfair for any reason you can dispute this with the agent. All things are usually negotiable. If you think that a charge is unreasonably high try to come to a fair compromise.

The landlord will also have a copy of the report – he too is free to discuss any items he feels are incorrect. The agent will not normally release your deposit until an agreement, by all parties, is reached.

Many tenants are shocked when they finally receive what is left of their security deposit. Charges for damage/cleaning at the end of the tenancy can quickly add up. On page 139 is an example of a typical Condition Report made after 'checking-out' some tenants on behalf of a letting agent. Take a look at the costs. This could be *your* deposit. With a little preparation and care you could save yourself a lot of money.

CHECK-OUT REPORT

RE: 9 ANY COURT, READING

Agent/Landlord:

Date of Check-out: 26.4.20XX

Meter Readings: Electricity – Low 77720 Normal 34864
                          Ref: K88C00478

Gas: N/A

Forwarding Address: 16 The Street, Chichester, Sussex

Telephone No: 07783 194832

Keys Handed Back: 2 Security door, 2 Yale front, 2 Chubb
                          front, plus 2 parking permits as listed.

Collected by: (Signature)

Windows & Doors   Yes
Secured:

Burglar Alarm: N/A

Telephone: Disconnected

Heating/Water: Off

GENERAL CONDITION

House: The property has been left in a clean condition with
          minor damage

Garden: Some tidying needed – borders weedy and grass
          needs cutting

Inspection Findings and   **Cost of Proposed Deductions**
Action Required

(To be continued on back of form if necessary)

Landlord's Signature (or his representative) ....

Tenant's Signature ....

Dated ....

Sample Condition Report

Details	Action	Cost
Front garden: grass long, borders weedy	Gardener to attend	£45.00 (3 hours)
Hall carpet: grubby marks	To be cleaned	£45.00
All skirtings dusty and doors grubby	To be cleaned	£30.00 (2 hours)
Window sills in lounge and kitchen stained and scratched	Make good	£35.00
Kitchen: requires cleaning throughout (including appliances) (oven cleaning is an additional charge of around £60)	To be cleaned	£65.00
Missing: 4 wine glasses, 2 plates, 1 cereal bowl	Replace at cost	£15.00

Handling Disputes

If you feel you have been unfairly treated or are being grossly overcharged for damage, you should write to your agent setting out the reasons why you should not be charged so much. Be realistic, compare the check-out comments against your copy of the inventory; if there is a case for complaint you should seek professional advice immediately and state your intentions in writing to the agent or landlord.

Your letting agent will often quote that as far as your check-out goes 'the inventory clerk's word is final'. This is a common misunderstanding and is actually not correct under European law. If push comes to shove, in the British Law Courts it will not necessarily be the case here either. This phrase pops up again and again and is sometimes included on the declaration that you are asked to sign on the back page of the inventory when you move in.

While it is true that it is the inventory clerk who will carry out the check-out inspection and produce a report of his findings, sometimes this is by no means final. Your landlord has as much input to the resulting charges on this report as the inventory company and the letting agent. This could leave you, the tenant, a little exposed financially. Nine out of ten deposit returns are fairly straightforward and, of course, a tenant must take full responsibility for any damage or cleaning they have incurred – but no more than this.

The most dangerous circumstance for a tenant moving out is when the landlord is about to move back into his property. He will arrive and suddenly think that the place was in a much better condition at the start of the tenancy than it really was, finding all sorts of things to try and pin on the outgoing tenant. Over the years, I have dealt with landlords who wanted anything from complete redecoration throughout to new carpets and appliances to be paid for by the tenants after they had moved out. In fact, some of them wanted their property to be in better condition than when the tenancy started! This is clearly unfair and unjust.

Letting agents need to be firm with their client, the landlord. Sadly, this is not always the case. If you have already seen your check-out report and suddenly major expenses are added that you know nothing about, you will need to discuss this immediately with the agent before any money is deducted from your deposit. This is another really good reason why the landlord should not hold your deposit from the start. By keeping your money in a separate client's account the agent has acted as 'stake-holder'; that means an independent, unbiased representative who is bonded to take care of your money until all disputes are resolved at the end of the tenancy. In this capacity he should not release any part of your deposit to the landlord without your permission.

It will be in your best interests to make the inventory clerk your new 'best friend'. As it is the clerk's opinion that counts at this stage, if he is on your side and thinks that the landlord's demands are unfair, he will be prepared to back this up with any documentation you require. He will also, for a fee, be able to attend a court of law to help you in your case should this be necessary.

If you have to deal directly with your landlord this could be more difficult. I have occasionally come across landlords who are real 'push-overs' when it comes to the check-out. They can be very laid back about it all and not be too fussy so long as their property has been left in a clean and tidy condition with no major damage. I have known these kinds of landlords actually to bring their cheque book along to the check-out and return the tenant's deposit straightaway. This is very unusual of course. By the end of the tenancy you will know what kind of landlord you are dealing with. From experience, it's more likely that your landlord will not be this easy to deal with. You must make sure that you meet him for the check-out inspection and then you will have the opportunity to discuss any problems or items for which he intends to charge you money. If you are hit with a big bill for things that you feel are not your responsibility, you should write to or call your landlord and ask for a full explanation of his charges to your deposit. Keep copies of all correspondence and make a note of time, date and content of phone calls. Always try to negotiate before you threaten court action. You might be able to reach a compromise and save yourself a lot of time and worry. Never forget the power of communication; if you don't ask, you don't get.

Your landlord or agent should then provide you with a full explanation, backed up by documentary evidence such as paid invoices from a cleaning company or for replacement of any broken items. If you are certain that you are being charged unfairly then you have one further choice: legal action.

Your letter could look something like this:

62 Mornington Road
Hounslow
Middlesex TW6 8AY
01734 868222

16 October 20XX

Mr Bill Watts
18 High Road
Hounslow
Middlesex TW6 9EX

Dear Mr Watts

Re: (address of your rented property)

I rented your property at the above address from 10 January 20XX to 10 September 20XX with a security deposit, held by you, of £1,200. I have now received your cheque for the return of this deposit and note that you have deducted a total of £800 for cleaning and damage. I feel that this is an unfair amount and ask that you provide a full explanation within seven days of the date of this letter. If this is not forthcoming, I will be taking legal action to recover my deposit. I await your reply.

Yours sincerely

You should also contact TDS (The Dispute Service) – see Useful Contacts on page 150 – who can act as arbitrators and order that your deposit is held by them until any dispute is resolved.

Small Claims Procedure

Your other course of action, if you feel you have been charged for items for which you weren't responsible, is to sue your landlord through the small claims court.

This is a relatively simple procedure and covers claims against a company or an individual in England and Wales up to a maximum of £5,000. Proceedings are held in the County Court. You should ring the court and ask for three copies of Form N1 – this is free. You will need three copies: one for you, one for the court and one for the person you are claiming from (your landlord). The court will post to the defendant a copy of the claim and a response pack: forms for use in reply to your claim. He is given fourteen days in which to reply. If your landlord just ignores this situation, you can ask the court to enter a judgment by default.

If a person has no other income or is bankrupt you could be out of luck. Even if you get a judgment in your favour it is no guarantee that you will be paid what is due to you. If this happens you can ask the court to enforce the judgment.

You can also talk to your local Citizens Advice Bureau; contact details can be found in your local telephone directory, library or from directory enquiries. The CAB has experience in all kinds of tenants' problems and their advice is free of charge. Their trained staff can offer advice about your rights as a tenant. They can help with writing letters and with information about the small claims court procedure if this is deemed necessary.

Remember, if you feel you have a strong case and that your deposit is being withheld unfairly, you should always seek legal advice immediately.

Release of Your Deposit

While any discussions or legal action are taking place it is not usually necessary for the agent to hold on to your security deposit in its entirety. It is common practice, but not necessarily known to the poor tenants, that the un-disputed part of the deposit can generally be released back to the tenant. For example, if the deposit held is £1,000 and there is a dispute at the end of the tenancy concerning the cost of replacing a carpet for £250, the agent can simply keep this amount of money and return the balance, £750, to the tenant. If, at a later date, the dispute is resolved, either by mutual agreement or by a court of law, the remaining £250 can then be refunded or used to cover the agreed charges. It is obviously better for the tenant to receive the larger undisputed part of his deposit rather than the whole amount being held by the agent for what could be several months.

Case History

A group of four students moved out of their house in Wales and their landlord had been quite unhelpful for the whole of their one-year tenancy. When it came to handing back their deposit they received a short letter saying that they were to receive nothing at all as the house needed cleaning and there was damage to pay for. One of the group had taken the precaution of writing detailed comments on the inventory at the start so took some professional advice. He then wrote a carefully worded and factual letter to the landlord pointing out the condition listed and agreed on the inventory and stating that if the deposit was not returned within the next seven days, he would look forward to meeting the landlord in the small claims court! Backed up by the written evidence, the landlord realised that he did not have a case so returned the whole deposit.

For those occasions when problems arise there is usually a solution, so long as you have written evidence from the start of the tenancy and any other written evidence acquired during your time in the property to cover any changes or other events.

Successful Tenancies – A Final Thought
With the cost of buying a first property becoming more
and more prohibitive the lettings sector can only grow.
Becoming a tenant is a necessary but expensive business
whichever way you look at it. The whole process need not
be fraught with problems and with the information you
now have from this book, I hope that your own renting
experience will be a safe and happy one.

Information empowers. You now have a good insight
into the whole business of renting and should be able to
protect yourself and your money from the worst problems
that can occur during normal tenancies. Always bear in
mind though that if you do experience any serious problems you should seek professional or legal advice.

FREQUENTLY ASKED QUESTIONS

Q. I have been asked by the landlord to move out of the property I rent as he wants to carry out some major repairs. This will make the house uninhabitable for a while. What can I do?

A. The landlord may have to provide you with some alternative accommodation while the work is being carried out. If you refuse to leave he can get a court order to repossess the property. You should seek some independent advice from a qualified adviser.

Q. I cannot afford to pay my rent and my friend wants to move in but the landlord has refused to allow this. Can my friend just move in anyway?

A. If you allow this, without permission, you will be in breach of your tenancy agreement and the landlord will have grounds to evict you should he choose.

Q. We are paying the landlord directly for the electricity bill and because we are late with our rent payments he has had the supply cut off, is this legal?

A. No, your landlord cannot lawfully arrange for disconnection of your electricity supply. You should contact the electricity company and ask to have the account put in your name to enable you to pay them direct or contact your local Environmental Health Department or Citizens Advice Bureau for advice.

Q. **The electric cooker in our property keeps sparking and I think it's unsafe. The landlord ignores our calls; what can I do?**

A. Your landlord is legally responsible for ensuring that his electrical appliances are safe. Contact the local office of the Health and Safety Executive (HSE) who have a duty to enforce all safety requirements.

Q. **A small crack has appeared in the edge of our bath right against the hand-grip. Am I responsible and will I be charged later?**

A. If the crack has appeared very close to the grip this should be a normal wear-and-tear issue and is usually caused by a stress fracture. However, you must report this damage straightaway by telephone and in writing to whoever is managing the property.

Q. **We moved into an unfurnished property and can't maintain the garden as no garden tools were supplied. Are we responsible for mowing the grass?**

A. Whether or not the landlord supplied a lawn mower, it is still your responsibility to keep the garden tidy. If you don't you will be in breach of your tenancy agreement.

Q. **I have left my job and will be working from home. Do I need to tell my landlord?**

A. There may be a clause in your tenancy agreement that forbids using the property as a place of business. In reality, however, if you are simply using one room as an office this should not be a problem. It is courteous to check with your landlord that this is acceptable.

USEFUL CONTACTS

Association of Independent Inventory Clerks (AIIC)
AIIC Central Office
Willow House
16 Commonfields
West End
Woking
Surrey GU24 9HZ
Tel/Fax: 01276 855388
E-mail: centraloffice@aiic.uk.com
www.aiic.uk.com
A useful website which lists professional inventory clerks around the UK and gives helpful advice for landlords and tenants.

Association of Residential Letting Agents (ARLA)
Maple House
53-55 Woodside Road
Amersham
Buckinghamshire HP6 6AA
Tel: 0845 3455752
Fax: 01494 431530
E-mail: info@arla.co.uk
www.arla.co.uk
A national association which provides several levels of recognised training for the industry. Also provides advice and information.

Citizens Advice Bureau
www.citizensadvice.org.uk
www.adviceguide.org.uk
Provides expert and free advice on any number of problems. Ring your local branch for an appointment.

Department of Trade & Industry
The Consumer Safety Unit
Room 302
10-18 Victoria Street
London SW1H 0NN
www.dti.gov.uk

Health & Safety Executive
For any health and safety issues, check your telephone directory for your local office or there is a free 24-hour Gas Safety Advice Line: 0800 300363

National Association of Estate Agents (NAEA)
Arbon House
21 Jury Street
Warwick CV34 4EH
Tel: 01926 496800
E-mail: info@naea.co.uk
www.naea.co.uk

TDS Ltd (The Dispute Service)
PO Box 541
Amersham
Buckinghamshire
HP6 6ZR
Tel: 0845 226 7837
Fax: 01494 431123
E-mail: deposits@tds.gb.com
www.tds.gb.com

Television Licensing
Tel: 08705 763763

More Useful Websites

www.lettings-landlords.co.uk
Some useful free information but there is a membership
fee for full access and advice.

www.nalscheme.co.uk
A membership association for letting agents; members
adhere to set standards of practice. Some helpful information for both landlords and tenants.

www.nusonline.co.uk
The National Union of Students' website with lots of
online information and links to sites covering most student
requirements including housing matters.

SAMPLE ASSURED SHORTHOLD TENANCY AGREEMENT

Please note the following is an example for information only and should not be used as a legal document without seeking professional/legal advice.

For letting a dwelling house on an Assured Shorthold Tenancy under Part 1 of the Housing Act 1988 as amended by the Housing Act 1996

This Agreement is made on the .... day of .... 20.....

Between: (the landlord) ....

Of: ....

And: (the tenants) ....

Of: ....

1.1 The landlord lets and the tenant takes the property, together with furniture, fixtures, fittings and effects also outbuildings and gardens (as appropriate) known as:
(address of property to be let)
for the term at the rent payable according to the terms and conditions of this agreement.

The Term

1.2 This Agreement is intended to create an Assured Shorthold Tenancy as defined by Part 1 of the Housing Act 1988.

1.3 The term shall be for the period of .... from and including (start date) to and including (finish date).

1.4 Should the tenant remain in the property beyond the end of the initial fixed term the tenant will have a Statutory Periodic Tenancy under Section 5 of the Housing Act 1988.

   (a) The tenant may bring the tenancy to an end before the expiry of the fixed term by giving the landlord or his agent at least two months' notice in writing but not within six months of the commencement date.

   (b) The landlord may bring the tenancy to an end at any time before the expiry of the fixed term by giving the tenant at least two months' written notice, or notice under section 21 of the Housing Act 1988, but not within six months of the commencement date.

The Rental Payments

1.5 The rent shall be (monthly rent amount) per calendar month, payable in advance on the .... day of each month. The first of these payments to be made on the signing of this contract.

1.6 The rent shall be paid by standing order, clear of all deductions whatsoever, to such bank as the landlord or his managing agent may nominate. If the said rent is not paid within seven days of becoming due interest will be charged at the rate of 4 per cent above base rate from the due day until the date payment is received.

Deposit

1.7   A deposit of £XXX shall be paid by the tenant to be held by the landlord's agent as stakeholder. This sum to be applied against breakages, damage, or non-performance of the terms of this agreement at the discretion of the managing agent and in no circumstances to be treated by the tenant as rent otherwise to be returned in full without interest but without prejudice to the landlord's right to claim full compensation in the event of the said deposit not being adequate to compensate him.

1.8   At the end of the tenancy, should deductions be made, the balance of the deposit will be refunded within twenty-one days to the persons so named on this Agreement.

1.9   The tenant hereby agrees with the landlord:

(a)   To pay the rent on the day and in the manner specified.

(b)   To pay for all gas, electricity, telephone and water charges which are due for supplies to the property during the tenancy.

(c)   Not to make any alterations or additions to the premises nor to damage or injure the same, nor to drive any nails into walls without the prior written consent of the landlord, such consent shall not be unreasonably withheld.

(d) Not to cause nuisance or annoyance to the landlord or to tenants/occupiers of adjoining premises, or to cause anything which may invalidate the landlord's insurance.

(e) To preserve and keep clean the interior of the premises including fixtures and fittings and to prevent destruction and damage of the landlord's said property.

(f) To ensure that the property is left properly secured at all times and if left unoccupied for a period of more than thirty days to take all necessary precautions to protect the heating and water systems during periods of cold weather and to inform the landlord or his agent.

(g) Not to remove any of the landlord's furniture, fixtures and effects from the premises and to leave all items in the same positions in the property at the end of the term.

(h) Not to keep any animals in or outside of the premises without the landlord's express consent.

(i) Not to carry on any business or profession from the premises or to receive paying guests without the landlord's written consent.

(j) Not to alter the general character of the garden, keep all drains clear, replace any broken glass, replace tap washers, keep guttering clear and down pipes free running.

(k) Notify the landlord immediately of any repairs necessary during the tenancy; negligence that

causes further damage to the landlord's property will cause the tenant to be penalised at the
end of the term.

(l)   To permit the landlord and/or his agent access
at all reasonable times by appointment during
the tenancy to enter into the premises for the
purpose of repairing or carrying out any works
necessary.

(m)   To permit reasonable access, by appointment,
during the last six weeks of the tenancy for the
purpose of viewing by prospective tenants or for
other purposes that the landlord may require.

(n)   To yield up the premises at the end of the
tenancy with all furniture, fixtures and fittings
in the same clean condition as they were at the
commencement of the term. To make good or
pay for repair or replacement of such items that
shall be broken, lost, damaged or destroyed
during the tenancy. Reasonable wear and tear
excepted.

(o)   To purchase the appropriate television licence;
and all mail delivered to the property which is
not addressed to the tenant's name herein,
should be redirected to the landlord or his
agent.

(p)   Not to change locks or supply additional locks
anywhere in the property without the landlord's
express permission.

(q)   Not to have fitted any aerial, antennae or satel-
lite dish to the building without the landlord's
express permission.

1.10 The landlord hereby agrees with the tenant:

(a) To pay and indemnify the tenant against all taxes, rates, assessment and outgoings in respect of the property except charges for the supply of gas, oil, electricity, water, telephone and council tax.

(b) To allow the tenant, paying rent, quiet enjoyment of the property without unlawful interruption from the landlord or any person claiming under or in trust for the landlord.

(c) To return to the tenant any rent paid for any period while the property is rendered uninhabitable by fire or other risk for which the landlord has agreed to insure, except where such damage may have been caused or enabled by the tenant's actions or omissions.

(d) To maintain the property and outbuildings throughout the term in reasonable repair and to replace any of the said fixtures, furniture and fittings which shall become irreparable by reason of fair wear and tear.

(e) That he is the sole owner of the leasehold or freehold interest in the property and that all necessary consents have been obtained in writing to allow him to enter this Agreement.

AS WITNESS THE HANDS OF THE SAID PARTIES:

LANDLORD (name) ....

SIGNATURE ....

IN THE PRESENCE OF (witness signature) ....

PRINT NAME ....

ADDRESS ....

TENANT (name) ....

SIGNATURE ....

DATED THIS DAY OF ....

IN THE YEAR OF ....

INDEX